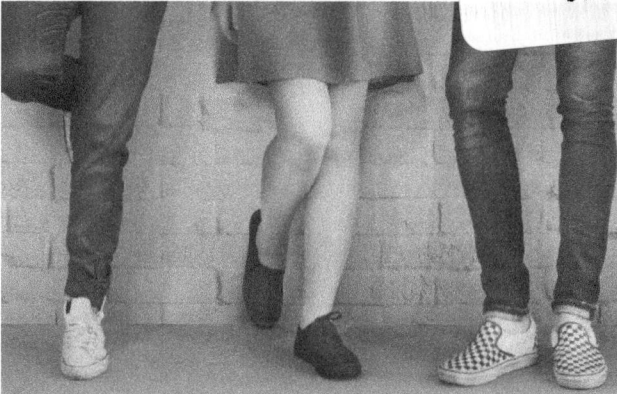

Let no one look down on your youth, but be an example for
the believers in speech, in conduct, in love, in faith, in purity.
1 Timothy 4:12

40 DAYS
DEVOTIONAL
FOR YOUTHS

COMING-OF-AGE IN CHRIST

EDWARD D. ANDREWS

40 DAYS DEVOTIONAL FOR YOUTHS

Coming-of-Age In Christ

Edward D. Andrews

Christian Publishing House

Cambridge, Ohio

CHRISTIAN PUBLISHING HOUSE

CONSERVATIVE CHRISTIAN BOOKS

APOLOGETIC DEFENSE OF GOD, THE
FAITH, THE BIBLE, AND CHRISTIANITY

40 DAYS DEVOTIONAL FOR YOUTHS Coming-of-Age In Christ by Edward D. Andrews

ISBN-13: 978-1-945757-59-4

ISBN-10: 1-945757-59-0

Table of Content

Book Description

"40 Days Devotional for Youths: Coming-of-Age In Christ" is a powerful and inspiring book that challenges young Christians to deepen their faith and relationship with God. This devotional is designed to guide readers through 40 days of reflection, prayer, and spiritual growth, helping them to navigate the challenges and opportunities of their teenage years.

With a focus on key themes such as identity, purpose, and relationships, this devotional offers practical insights and biblical wisdom that will help young people to develop a strong and lasting faith. Each day features a scripture reading, a devotional reflection, and a series of questions and prompts for reflection and prayer. The devotions are written in a relatable and engaging style, making them perfect for teenagers and young adults.

Throughout the book, readers will explore important topics such as self-image, forgiveness, and the power of community. They will also learn valuable lessons about the importance of prayer, service, and living a life that reflects God's love and grace.

Whether you're a teenager who is just starting to explore your faith, or a young adult who is looking for a fresh perspective on your spiritual journey, "40 Days Devotional for Youths: Coming-of-Age In Christ" is the perfect resource to help you grow in your relationship with God. With its engaging style, practical insights, and powerful message of hope and grace, this devotional is sure to become an essential part of your spiritual journey.

Preface

Dear reader,

Thank you for picking up "40 Days Devotional for Youths: Coming-of-Age In Christ". This book is a reflection of my heart for young people and their spiritual growth. As a Christian and a youth leader, I have seen firsthand the challenges and opportunities that young people face in their teenage years. I have also seen the transformative power of faith and the impact it can have on the lives of young people.

The purpose of this book is to provide young people with a practical and accessible guide to growing in their faith and deepening their relationship with God. I have designed this devotional to be read over a period of 40 days, with each day focusing on a different topic or theme. Each day features a scripture reading, a devotional reflection, and a series of questions and prompts for reflection and prayer.

As you journey through this devotional, my hope is that you will be inspired, encouraged, and challenged in your faith. I pray that you will come to know God more deeply, and that you will discover the purpose and calling that He has for your life. I also hope that this devotional will be a resource for you as you navigate the challenges and opportunities of your teenage years, and that it will provide you with practical insights and biblical wisdom to help you grow in your relationship with God.

May this devotional be a blessing to you on your spiritual journey, and may you come to experience the transformative power of faith and the love of God in your life.

Blessings,

Edward D. Andrews

Introduction

Welcome to "40 Days Devotional for Youths: Coming-of-Age In Christ". This devotional is designed to help young people deepen their faith and relationship with God as they navigate the challenges and opportunities of their teenage years. Whether you are just starting to explore your faith or you are looking for a fresh perspective on your spiritual journey, this devotional is for you.

As a Christian and a youth leader, I have seen firsthand the struggles and questions that young people face as they seek to understand their identity, purpose, and place in the world. That's why I have created this devotional, to provide practical and biblical insights that will help young people grow in their faith and discover the transformative power of God's love and grace.

This devotional is organized into 40 days, with each day focusing on a different theme or topic. Each day features a scripture reading, a devotional reflection, and a series of questions and prompts for reflection and prayer. The topics covered in this devotional include identity, purpose, relationships, prayer, service, forgiveness, and more.

Throughout this devotional, my hope is that you will come to know God more deeply, and that you will discover the purpose and calling that He has for your life. I also hope that this devotional will be a resource for you as you navigate the challenges and opportunities of your teenage years, and that it will provide you with practical insights and biblical wisdom to help you grow in your relationship with God.

May this devotional be a source of encouragement, inspiration, and hope for you on your spiritual journey. May you come to know God more deeply and experience the transformative power of His love and grace in your life.

DAY 1 The Promise of God's Faithfulness in Times of Temptation

1 Corinthians 10:13 Updated American Standard Version (UASV)

[13] No temptation has overtaken you but such as is common to man; and God is faithful, who will not allow you to be tempted beyond what you are able, but with the temptation will provide the way of escape also, so that you will be able to endure it.

Commentary

1 Corinthians 10:13 is a well-known verse that offers encouragement to Christians facing trials and temptations. In this verse, Paul assures the Corinthian believers that God is faithful and will not allow them to be tempted beyond what they can bear. Instead, He will provide a way out so that they can endure the temptation.

This verse is particularly relevant in our daily lives, as we all face various trials and temptations. Whether it's a struggle with addiction, a difficult relationship, or a challenging circumstance, we can take comfort in the fact that God is with us and will provide a way out. It's important to note, however, that God's provision doesn't always mean that He will remove us from the situation. Instead, He may give us the strength, wisdom, and discernment we need to resist temptation and overcome our trials.

One of the key themes of this verse is the faithfulness of God. We can trust that God will keep His promises and will always be there for us, no matter what we are going through. In times of temptation and trial, we can turn to God for strength and find hope in His faithfulness.

Overall, 1 Corinthians 10:13 is a powerful reminder that we are not alone in our struggles. God is with us, and He will provide a way out so that we can endure and overcome the challenges we face.

Devotional for Youths

As teenagers, we face many challenges and temptations every day. Whether it's peer pressure, social media, or personal struggles, it can be easy to feel overwhelmed and discouraged. However, as followers of Christ, we have a promise of hope in 1 Corinthians 10:13. God is faithful, and He will not allow us to be tempted beyond what we can bear. Not only that, but He will provide a way out so that we can endure it.

But what does this mean for us practically? How can we overcome temptation with God's faithfulness?

Firstly, we need to recognize that we are not alone in our struggles. We are all human, and we all face temptation. It's important to talk to trusted friends or mentors about what we're going through and to ask for help and support. We can also turn to God in prayer and ask for His strength and guidance.

Secondly, we need to be proactive in avoiding situations that may lead us into temptation. For example, if we struggle with a certain sin or addiction, we should avoid places or activities that may trigger those desires. Instead, we can find healthy and positive ways to occupy our time and focus on God's plan for our lives.

Lastly, we need to trust in God's faithfulness and His promise to provide a way out. This may not always look like an immediate solution, but it could come in the form of increased self-control, wisdom, or discernment. We can also trust that God is using our struggles to shape us and mold us into the person He wants us to be.

So today, let's hold on to the promise of 1 Corinthians 10:13. Let's remember that God is faithful, and He will help us overcome temptation. We are not alone in our struggles, and we can trust in His provision and guidance. Let's pray for His strength and wisdom as we face each day with hope and confidence in Him.

DAY 2 Finding Courage in God's Presence and Protection

Deuteronomy 31:6 Updated American Standard Version (UASV)

⁶ Be strong and courageous. Do not fear or be in dread of them, for it is Jehovah your God who goes with you. He will not leave you or forsake you."

Commentary

Deuteronomy 31:6 is a verse that provides comfort and encouragement to God's people in times of uncertainty and difficulty. In this verse, Moses is speaking to the Israelites as they prepare to enter the Promised Land. He encourages them to be strong and courageous, reminding them that Jehovah their God will never leave them or forsake them.

This verse is a powerful reminder of God's faithfulness and presence in the lives of His people. It shows us that even in the midst of difficult circumstances, we can trust in God's protection and guidance. We don't need to be afraid or discouraged, because God is with us and will never abandon us.

This verse is also a call to action. Moses is telling the Israelites to be strong and courageous, implying that they will face challenges and difficulties as they enter the Promised Land. However, he is also reminding them that they can overcome these challenges with God's help. They don't need to rely on their own strength or abilities but can instead rely on the power of God.

For Christians today, this verse is just as relevant. We too face challenges and difficulties in our lives, but we can trust in God's presence and protection. We don't need to be afraid or discouraged, because God is with us. We can also find strength and courage in the knowledge that we are not alone in our struggles, but that God is with us every step of the way.

Overall, Deuteronomy 31:6 is a powerful reminder of God's faithfulness and presence in the lives of His people. It is a call to action, urging us to be strong and courageous in the face of difficulties and challenges, knowing that God is with us and will never abandon us.

Devotional for Youth

As teenagers, we face many challenges and uncertainties in our lives. Whether it's school, relationships, or our future plans, it can be easy to feel overwhelmed and discouraged. However, as followers of Christ, we have a promise of hope in Deuteronomy 31:6. God is with us, and He will never leave us or forsake us.

But how can we find courage in God's presence and protection? How can we overcome our fears and uncertainties and trust in Him?

Firstly, we need to recognize that we are not alone in our struggles. God is with us, and He will never abandon us. We can turn to Him in prayer and ask for His guidance and strength. We can also seek out the support and encouragement of our Christian community, whether that's our church, youth group, or close friends.

Secondly, we need to be intentional in our relationship with God. This means spending time in prayer and reading the Bible, and actively seeking out His will for our lives. As we draw closer to God, we will begin to understand His character and His promises, and we will be better equipped to trust in Him and find courage in His presence.

Lastly, we need to have a mindset of faith and trust. This means choosing to believe in God's promises, even when we can't see how they will be fulfilled. It means choosing to have courage in the face of our fears and uncertainties, knowing that God is with us and will never abandon us.

So today, let's hold on to the promise of Deuteronomy 31:6. Let's remember that God is with us, and He will never leave us or forsake us. Let's seek out His guidance and strength, and trust in

His presence and protection. Let's have courage in the face of our fears and uncertainties, knowing that we can find hope and peace in Him.

DAY 3 The Power of Our Words: Speaking Truth in Love

Ephesians 4:29 Updated American Standard Version (UASV)

[29] Let no corrupting talk come out of your mouths, but only such as is good for building up, as the need may be, that it may give grace to those who hear.

Commentary

Ephesians 4:29 is a verse that reminds us of the power of our words and the importance of using them to build up and encourage others. In this verse, Paul urges the Ephesian believers to only speak what is good and helpful, and to use their words to bring grace to those who hear them.

This verse is particularly relevant in our modern world, where communication has become easier and more widespread than ever before. With social media, texting, and other forms of instant messaging, we have a constant stream of words and messages flowing in and out of our lives. It's easy to get caught up in negativity, criticism, and gossip, but Paul reminds us that our words have the power to shape our lives and the lives of those around us.

One of the key themes of this verse is the importance of edifying speech. We are called to use our words to build up and encourage others, rather than tearing them down or speaking negative things about them. This means speaking truth in love, offering words of affirmation, and avoiding harmful or hurtful speech.

Another important theme of this verse is the idea of grace. Our words should not only be good and helpful, but they should also bring grace to those who hear them. This means offering forgiveness, understanding, and kindness to others, even when they may not deserve it. It means reflecting the grace and love of Christ in our words and actions.

Overall, Ephesians 4:29 is a powerful reminder of the importance of our words and the impact they can have on the world around us. It challenges us to be mindful of what we say and how we say it, and to use our words to build up and encourage others. It also reminds us of the power of grace and the importance of reflecting Christ's love in everything we say and do.

Devotional for Youth

As teenagers, we have a lot of words and messages coming in and out of our lives. We use social media, texting, and other forms of communication to connect with friends and family, express our opinions, and share our experiences. However, in the midst of all this noise, it can be easy to forget the power of our words and the impact they can have on others.

In Ephesians 4:29, Paul reminds us of the importance of using our words to build up and encourage others. He urges us to avoid unwholesome talk and to only speak what is helpful and beneficial to those who listen. This means speaking truth in love, offering words of affirmation, and avoiding harmful or hurtful speech.

But why is this so important? Why do our words matter?

Firstly, our words have the power to shape our lives and the lives of those around us. The words we speak can either build up or tear down, and they can have a lasting impact on how others perceive us and how we perceive ourselves. When we use our words to build up and encourage others, we are reflecting the love and grace of Christ in our lives.

Secondly, our words have the power to influence our thoughts and emotions. When we speak positively and truthfully, we can uplift ourselves and those around us. However, when we speak negatively or hurtfully, we can cause ourselves and others to feel discouraged, hurt, or angry.

Lastly, our words have the power to reflect our faith and our relationship with God. As Christians, we are called to love others as Christ loves us. This means using our words to build up and encourage others, to speak truth in love, and to reflect the grace and love of Christ in all that we say and do.

So today, let's remember the power of our words. Let's strive to speak truth in love, and to use our words to build up and encourage those around us. Let's seek out opportunities to reflect the grace and love of Christ in everything we say and do, and let's trust in the power of our words to make a positive impact on the world around us.

DAY 4 Honoring Our Parents: A Call to Gratitude and Respect

Exodus 20:12 Updated American Standard Version (UASV)

¹² "Honor your father and your mother, that your days may be prolonged in the land which Jehovah your God gives you.

Commentary

Exodus 20:12 is one of the Ten Commandments given by God to Moses on Mount Sinai. This commandment instructs us to honor our parents, so that we may have a long and prosperous life.

At its core, this commandment is about showing respect and gratitude to those who have raised us and cared for us. It is a call to recognize the sacrifices that our parents have made for us, and to honor their wisdom and guidance.

This commandment also has broader implications for our relationships with others. It teaches us the importance of showing respect and honor to those in authority over us, whether that's our parents, teachers, or employers. By treating others with respect and honor, we can create a culture of mutual respect and trust.

In addition, this commandment reminds us of the importance of family and community. When we honor our parents and show gratitude for their guidance, we are building stronger bonds within our family and creating a sense of connection and belonging. This can also extend to our relationships with others, as we seek to build strong and supportive communities.

Overall, Exodus 20:12 is a powerful reminder of the importance of showing respect and honor to those who have cared for us and guided us in life. It is a call to recognize the sacrifices that our parents have made for us, and to honor their wisdom and guidance. It also has broader implications for our relationships with others and for building stronger, more supportive communities.

Devotional for Youth

As teenagers, we are constantly seeking to define ourselves and our place in the world. We often focus on our relationships with our peers and friends, while overlooking the importance of our relationship with our parents. However, as Christians, we are called to honor and respect our parents, recognizing the sacrifices they have made for us and the wisdom they have to offer.

In Exodus 20:12, God commands us to honor our father and mother, so that we may live long in the land He has given us. This commandment is not just about showing respect and gratitude to our parents, but it is also a call to recognize the important role they play in our lives.

So, how can we honor our parents in practical ways?

Firstly, we can show gratitude. We can thank our parents for the sacrifices they have made for us and for their constant love and support. We can express our appreciation for the wisdom and guidance they offer us, and we can seek their advice and input on important decisions.

Secondly, we can show respect. We can speak to our parents in a respectful and kind manner, even when we disagree with them. We can listen to their perspectives and try to understand where they are coming from, rather than dismissing their opinions.

Lastly, we can show love. We can prioritize our relationships with our parents and make time to spend with them. We can show them love and affection and offer them our support and encouragement.

Honoring our parents is not just a commandment, but it is also an opportunity to build stronger relationships and show gratitude for the blessings in our lives. As we seek to honor our parents, we can also learn valuable lessons about respect, love, and community, and grow in our faith and relationship with God.

So today, let's remember the commandment to honor our parents. Let's show gratitude, respect, and love to those who have cared for us and guided us in life. Let's seek to build stronger relationships and communities, and let's trust in God's provision and guidance as we honor those who have helped us along the way.

DAY 5 Persevering in Doing Good: Trusting in God's Timing and Provision

Galatians 6:9 Updated American Standard Version (UASV)

⁹ Let us not grow weary in doing good, for in due time we will reap if we do not grow weary.

Commentary

Galatians 6:9 is a verse that encourages believers to persevere in doing good, even when it may be difficult or discouraging. In this verse, Paul urges the Galatian church not to give up, but to keep sowing good seeds, knowing that they will reap a harvest if they do not give up.

This verse is particularly relevant in the context of the Galatian church, which was facing challenges and persecution. Paul reminds them that their efforts to do good are not in vain, and that God will reward their faithfulness.

This verse also has broader implications for our lives as believers. It reminds us of the importance of perseverance and the need to continue doing good, even in the face of adversity or discouragement. It also teaches us the importance of trusting in God's timing and provision, and not giving up on our faith or our commitment to following Christ.

Ultimately, Galatians 6:9 is a powerful reminder of the importance of faithfulness and perseverance in the Christian life. It encourages us to keep sowing good seeds, trusting in God's provision and timing, and knowing that our efforts to do good will ultimately be rewarded. By persevering in our faith and commitment to following Christ, we can experience the transformative power of God's love and grace in our lives.

Devotional for Youth

As teenagers, we face many challenges and opportunities in our lives. We may face peer pressure, academic stress, or uncertainty about our future. In the midst of these challenges, it can be easy to become discouraged or overwhelmed, and to lose sight of the importance of doing good and living out our faith.

However, in Galatians 6:9, Paul reminds us of the importance of perseverance and the need to continue doing good, even in the face of adversity or discouragement. He urges us not to become weary in doing good, but to trust in God's timing and provision, knowing that we will reap a harvest if we do not give up.

So how can we persevere in doing good, even when it may be difficult or discouraging?

Firstly, we can trust in God's provision. We can remember that God is faithful and that He will provide for us, even in the midst of our challenges and struggles. We can seek His guidance and strength in prayer, and trust that He will give us the wisdom and resources we need to continue doing good.

Secondly, we can surround ourselves with a community of support. We can seek out friends and mentors who share our values and can offer us encouragement and guidance. We can also find ways to serve and help others, as we seek to build a stronger and more supportive community.

Lastly, we can keep our focus on the ultimate goal. We can remember that our efforts to do good are not in vain, and that we will ultimately reap a harvest if we continue to sow good seeds. We can keep our focus on our faith and commitment to following Christ, trusting in His guidance and provision as we seek to live out His love and grace in the world around us.

So today, let's remember the importance of perseverance in doing good. Let's trust in God's timing and provision, and seek out the support of a strong and supportive community. Let's keep our focus on the ultimate goal, and trust in the transformative power of God's love and grace in our lives. May we continue to sow good seeds, knowing that we will ultimately reap a harvest if we do not give up.

DAY 6 Finding Strength in God's Presence and Protection

Isaiah 41:10 Updated American Standard Version (UASV)

[10] fear not, for I am with you;
    be not anxious, for I am your God;
I will strengthen you, I will help you,
    I will uphold you with my righteous right hand.

Commentary

Isaiah 41:10 is a powerful and comforting verse that reminds us of God's presence and protection in our lives. In this verse, God speaks through the prophet Isaiah to reassure His people, telling them not to be afraid, for He is with them and will uphold them with His righteous hand.

This verse is particularly relevant in the context of the book of Isaiah, which was written during a time of great upheaval and uncertainty for the Israelites. They were facing persecution and exile, and their faith was being tested in many ways. In this verse, God reminds them that they can trust in His presence and protection, even in the midst of their trials and difficulties.

This verse also has broader implications for our lives as believers. It reminds us that we can trust in God's faithfulness and provision, even in the face of our own challenges and uncertainties. It encourages us to turn to God in times of trouble, knowing that He will uphold us with His righteous hand and give us the strength and courage we need to face our challenges.

Ultimately, Isaiah 41:10 is a powerful reminder of God's love and care for His people. It reassures us that we are not alone in our struggles, and that we can trust in God's presence and protection, no matter what may come our way. By turning to God and trusting in His faithfulness, we can find hope and peace in the midst of our trials and difficulties.

Devotional for Youth

As teenagers, we face many challenges and uncertainties in our lives. We may be dealing with academic stress, peer pressure, or family difficulties. In the midst of these challenges, it can be easy to feel overwhelmed or discouraged, and to lose sight of the hope and strength that we have in Christ.

However, in Isaiah 41:10, God reassures us of His presence and protection, reminding us not to fear, but to trust in Him. He promises to strengthen and uphold us with His righteous hand, and to help us in all our difficulties.

So how can we find strength in God's presence and protection, even in the midst of our challenges?

Firstly, we can turn to God in prayer. We can seek His guidance and wisdom in our daily lives, and ask for His strength and protection in times of trouble. We can trust that God is always with us, and that He will help us in all our difficulties.

Secondly, we can find support in our Christian community. We can seek out friends and mentors who share our values and can offer us encouragement and guidance. We can also find ways to serve and help others, as we seek to build a stronger and more supportive community.

Lastly, we can keep our focus on God's promises. We can remember that God is faithful and that He will provide for us, even in the midst of our challenges and struggles. We can keep our focus on our faith and commitment to following Christ, trusting in His guidance and provision as we seek to live out His love and grace in the world around us.

So today, let's remember the comforting words of Isaiah 41:10. Let's turn to God in prayer, seeking His presence and protection in our daily lives. Let's find support in our Christian community, and seek out ways to serve and help others. And let's keep our focus on God's promises, trusting in His faithfulness and provision as we navigate the challenges and uncertainties of life.

May we find strength in God's presence and protection, knowing that He will always be with us and help us in all our difficulties.

DAY 7 Trusting in God's Plans: Finding Hope and Purpose in Life

Jeremiah 29:11 Updated American Standard Version (UASV)

[11] "'For I know the thoughts that I am thinking toward you,' declares Jehovah, 'thoughts of peace, and not of calamity, to give you a future and a hope.

Commentary

Jeremiah 29:11 is a well-known and beloved verse in the Bible. In this verse, God speaks through the prophet Jeremiah to reassure His people of His plans for them. He tells them that He has plans to prosper them and not to harm them, plans to give them hope and a future.

This verse is particularly relevant in the context of the book of Jeremiah, which was written during a time of great upheaval and uncertainty for the Israelites. They were facing persecution and exile, and their faith was being tested in many ways. In this verse, God reminds them that He has a purpose and a plan for their lives, and that they can trust in His provision and protection.

This verse also has broader implications for our lives as believers. It reminds us that God has a plan and a purpose for each of our lives, and that we can trust in His guidance and provision, even in the face of our own challenges and uncertainties. It encourages us to turn to God in times of trouble, knowing that He has a hope and a future for us that is greater than anything we could imagine.

Ultimately, Jeremiah 29:11 is a powerful reminder of God's love and care for His people. It reassures us that we are not alone in our struggles, and that we can trust in God's plans for our lives, no matter what may come our way. By turning to God and trusting in His guidance and provision, we can find hope and peace in the midst of our trials and difficulties.

Devotional for Youth

As teenagers, we often face a lot of uncertainty and questions about our future. We may be wondering what career path to pursue, what college to attend, or what our purpose in life is. It can be easy to become overwhelmed or discouraged, and to lose sight of the hope and purpose that we have in Christ.

However, in Jeremiah 29:11, God reminds us that He has a plan and a purpose for our lives. He tells us that His plans for us are to prosper us and not to harm us, to give us hope and a future. He encourages us to trust in His guidance and provision, knowing that He has a plan that is greater than anything we could imagine.

So how can we trust in God's plans and find hope and purpose in life?

Firstly, we can seek God's guidance and wisdom in prayer. We can ask for His help in discerning our purpose and direction in life, and trust that He will lead us on the right path. We can also seek the advice and guidance of others, such as trusted mentors or pastors, who can offer us wisdom and support.

Secondly, we can embrace opportunities for growth and learning. We can try new things, explore new interests, and seek out experiences that will help us grow and develop as individuals. We can trust that God will use these experiences to shape us and guide us on our journey.

Lastly, we can keep our focus on Christ and His calling for our lives. We can seek to serve and love others, and to live out His love and grace in the world around us. We can trust that by following His calling, we will find true fulfillment and purpose in life.

So today, let's remember the comforting words of Jeremiah 29:11. Let's seek God's guidance and wisdom in prayer, and trust in His plans and purposes for our lives. Let's embrace opportunities for growth and learning, and keep our focus on Christ and His calling for our lives. And let's find hope and purpose in knowing that God has a plan that is greater than anything we could imagine.

DAY 8 Living a Life of Purity: Finding Guidance in God's Word

Psalms 119:9 Updated American Standard Version (UASV)

⁹ How can a young man keep his way pure?
   By guarding it according to your word.

Commentary

Psalm 119:9 is a verse that emphasizes the importance of living a pure and righteous life before God. In this verse, the psalmist asks the question, "How can a young person stay on the path of purity?" and then answers it by saying, "By living according to your word."

This verse is particularly relevant in the context of the psalm as a whole, which is the longest chapter in the Bible and emphasizes the importance of following God's commandments and living a life of obedience and righteousness. The psalmist recognizes that it can be difficult for young people to stay on the path of purity, and emphasizes the importance of relying on God's word as a guide for righteous living.

This verse also has broader implications for our lives as believers. It reminds us that living a life of purity and righteousness is not always easy, but that we can rely on God's word to guide us and help us stay on the right path. It encourages us to prioritize our relationship with God and to seek His guidance and wisdom in all aspects of our lives.

Ultimately, Psalm 119:9 is a powerful reminder of the importance of living a life of purity and righteousness before God. It encourages us to turn to His word as a guide for righteous living, and to seek His guidance and wisdom as we navigate the challenges and temptations of life. By living according to His word, we can experience the transformative power of God's love and grace in our lives.

Devotional for Youth

As teenagers, we face many challenges and temptations in our lives. We may be tempted to compromise our values in order to fit in with our peers, or to pursue our own desires at the expense of our relationship with God. In the midst of these challenges, it can be easy to lose sight of the importance of living a life of purity and righteousness before God.

However, in Psalm 119:9, the psalmist reminds us of the importance of relying on God's word as a guide for righteous living. He asks the question, "How can a young person stay on the path of purity?" and answers it by saying, "By living according to your word." He encourages us to turn to God's word as a guide for our lives, and to seek His guidance and wisdom in all aspects of our lives.

So how can we live a life of purity and righteousness before God?

Firstly, we can prioritize our relationship with God. We can make time for prayer, worship, and Bible study, and seek to grow in our relationship with Him. We can ask for His guidance and wisdom in all aspects of our lives, trusting that He will lead us on the right path.

Secondly, we can seek out accountability and support. We can surround ourselves with friends and mentors who share our values and can offer us encouragement and guidance. We can also find ways to serve and help others, as we seek to live out our faith in tangible ways.

Lastly, we can keep our focus on God's calling for our lives. We can seek to use our talents and passions to glorify Him and to serve others, and to pursue His plans and purposes for our lives. We can trust that by living according to His word, we will experience the transformative power of His love and grace in our lives.

So today, let's remember the importance of living a life of purity and righteousness before God. Let's turn to His word as a guide for our lives and seek His guidance and wisdom in all aspects of our lives. Let's surround ourselves with accountability and support and seek out ways to serve and help others. And let's keep our focus on God's calling for our lives, trusting in His provision and guidance as we seek to live out our faith in the world around us.

DAY 9 Following God's Word: Finding Direction and Guidance for Life

Psalms 119:105 Updated American Standard Version (UASV)

[105] Your word is a lamp to my feet
and a light to my path.

Commentary

Psalm 119:105 is a verse that emphasizes the importance of God's word as a source of guidance and direction for our lives. In this verse, the psalmist writes, "Your word is a lamp for my feet, a light on my path."

This verse is particularly relevant in the context of the psalm as a whole, which is the longest chapter in the Bible and emphasizes the importance of following God's commandments and living a life of obedience and righteousness. The psalmist recognizes that God's word is a source of guidance and direction, providing light for the path of life.

This verse also has broader implications for our lives as believers. It reminds us that God's word is not just a collection of ancient writings, but a living and active guide for our lives. It encourages us to prioritize our relationship with God and to seek His guidance and wisdom in all aspects of our lives.

Ultimately, Psalm 119:105 is a powerful reminder of the importance of God's word in our lives. It encourages us to turn to His word as a source of guidance and direction, trusting in His wisdom and provision as we navigate the challenges and uncertainties of life. By following His word, we can experience the transformative power of His love and grace in our lives.

Devotional for Youth

As teenagers, we often face many decisions and uncertainties in our lives. We may be wondering what career path to pursue, what college to attend, or what our purpose in life is. In the midst of these uncertainties, it can be easy to feel lost or unsure of which direction to take.

However, in Psalm 119:105, the psalmist reminds us of the importance of God's word as a source of guidance and direction in our lives. He describes God's word as a lamp for our feet and a light on our path, emphasizing the role it plays in helping us find direction and purpose in life.

So how can we follow God's word and find direction and guidance for our lives?

Firstly, we can prioritize our relationship with God. We can make time for prayer, worship, and Bible study, seeking to grow in our knowledge and understanding of His word. We can ask for His guidance and wisdom in all aspects of our lives, trusting that He will lead us on the right path.

Secondly, we can seek out the guidance and wisdom of others. We can turn to trusted mentors, pastors, or friends for guidance and advice as we navigate the challenges of life. We can also seek out opportunities to serve and help others, recognizing that by serving others, we can gain a better understanding of God's plans and purposes for our lives.

Lastly, we can keep our focus on Christ and His calling for our lives. We can seek to use our talents and passions to serve Him and to bring glory to His name. We can trust that by following His word and living a life of obedience and righteousness, we will find true fulfillment and purpose in life.

So today, let's remember the importance of God's word as a source of guidance and direction for our lives. Let's prioritize our relationship with Him, seeking His guidance and wisdom in all aspects of our lives. Let's seek out the guidance and wisdom of others and find ways to serve and help those around us. And let's keep our focus on Christ and His calling for our lives, trusting in His provision and guidance as we seek to follow His word and live out His love in the world around us.

DAY 10 Finding Hope and Joy in God: Trusting in His Power

Romans 15:13 Updated American Standard Version (UASV)

[13] Now may the God of hope fill you with all joy and peace in believing, so that you will abound in hope by the power of the Holy Spirit.

Commentary

Romans 15:13 is a verse that emphasizes the importance of hope and joy in the lives of believers. In this verse, Paul writes, "May the God of hope fill you with all joy and peace as you trust in him, so that you may overflow with hope by the power of the Holy Spirit."

This verse is particularly relevant in the context of the book of Romans, which emphasizes the themes of faith, grace, and righteousness. Paul emphasizes the importance of trusting in God's grace and living a life of obedience and righteousness, and he reminds his readers of the hope and joy that comes from a life lived in faith.

This verse also has broader implications for our lives as believers. It reminds us that God is the source of our hope and joy, and that we can trust in Him to provide us with the strength and guidance we need to navigate the challenges of life. It encourages us to prioritize our relationship with God and to trust in His provision and guidance.

Ultimately, Romans 15:13 is a powerful reminder of the importance of hope and joy in our lives as believers. It reminds us that by trusting in God and living a life of faith, we can experience the transformative power of His love and grace in our lives. By relying on the power of the Holy Spirit, we can find true joy and peace, even in the midst of life's challenges and uncertainties.

Devotional for Youth

As teenagers, we often face many challenges and uncertainties in our lives. We may be struggling with academic or personal challenges or navigating the complexities of relationships and friendships. In the midst of these challenges, it can be easy to lose sight of the hope and joy that comes from a life lived in faith.

However, in Romans 15:13, Paul reminds us of the importance of trusting in God's power to fill us with hope and joy. He emphasizes the role that the Holy Spirit plays in our lives, providing us with the strength and guidance we need to navigate life's challenges and uncertainties.

So how can we find hope and joy in God and trust in His power?

Firstly, we can prioritize our relationship with God. We can make time for prayer, worship, and Bible study, seeking to grow in our knowledge and understanding of His love and grace. We can ask for His guidance and wisdom in all aspects of our lives, trusting that He will provide us with the strength and guidance we need to navigate life's challenges.

Secondly, we can seek out the guidance and support of others. We can turn to trusted mentors, pastors, or friends for guidance and support as we navigate the challenges of life. We can also seek out opportunities to serve and help others, recognizing that by serving others, we can experience the transformative power of God's love and grace in our lives.

Lastly, we can keep our focus on Christ and His calling for our lives. We can seek to use our talents and passions to serve Him and to bring glory to His name. We can trust that by following His will and living a life of faith, we will find true joy and peace, even in the midst of life's challenges and uncertainties.

So today, let's remember the importance of trusting in God's power to fill us with hope and joy. Let's prioritize our relationship with Him, seeking His guidance and wisdom in all aspects of our lives. Let's seek out the guidance and support of others, and find ways to serve and help those around us. And let's keep our focus on Christ and His calling for our lives, trusting in His provision and guidance as we seek to live out His love and grace in the world around us.

DAY 11 Finding Peace in Prayer: Trusting in God's Care

Philippians 4:6-7 Updated American Standard Version (UASV)

[6] In nothing be anxious; but in everything by prayer and supplication with thanksgiving let your requests be made known to God. [7] And the peace of God, which surpasses all understanding, will guard your hearts and your minds[1] in Christ Jesus.

Commentary

Philippians 4:6-7 is a powerful reminder of the importance of prayer and trust in the lives of believers. In these verses, Paul writes, "Do not be anxious about anything, but in every situation, by prayer and petition, with thanksgiving, present your requests to God. And the peace of God, which transcends all understanding, will guard your hearts and your minds in Christ Jesus."

These verses are particularly relevant in the context of Paul's letter to the Philippians, which emphasizes the themes of joy, contentment, and unity. Paul encourages his readers to rejoice in the Lord, to be content in all circumstances, and to seek unity and harmony with one another. He reminds them that through prayer and trust in God, they can experience the peace that surpasses all understanding.

This passage also has broader implications for our lives as believers. It reminds us that prayer and trust are powerful tools in navigating the challenges and uncertainties of life. It encourages us to turn to God in every situation, seeking His guidance and wisdom, and trusting in His provision and care for us.

Ultimately, Philippians 4:6-7 is a powerful reminder of the peace that comes from a life lived in faith and trust in God. It

---

[1] Or "your mental powers; your thoughts."

reminds us that by bringing our concerns and anxieties to God in prayer, we can experience His peace that surpasses all understanding, and find the strength and guidance we need to navigate life's challenges. By trusting in His provision and care for us, we can find true contentment and joy in every circumstance.

Devotional for Youth

As teenagers, we often face many worries and anxieties in our lives. We may be worried about school, friendships, or the future, and feel overwhelmed by the challenges we face. In the midst of these anxieties, it can be easy to lose sight of the peace and contentment that comes from a life lived in faith and trust in God.

However, in Philippians 4:6-7, Paul reminds us of the importance of prayer and trust in finding peace in every situation. He encourages us to bring our worries and anxieties to God in prayer, trusting in His provision and care for us.

So how can we find peace in prayer and trust in God's care?

Firstly, we can make prayer a priority in our lives. We can make time for prayer, seeking to grow in our relationship with God and to bring our concerns and worries to Him. We can ask for His guidance and wisdom in all aspects of our lives, trusting that He will provide us with the strength and guidance we need to navigate life's challenges.

Secondly, we can cultivate a spirit of thanksgiving in our lives. We can seek to focus on the blessings and goodness of God, and to give thanks for all that He has done for us. By cultivating a spirit of gratitude, we can find joy and contentment in every circumstance, and experience the peace that comes from knowing that God is with us.

Lastly, we can keep our focus on Christ and His calling for our lives. We can seek to use our talents and passions to serve Him and to bring glory to His name. We can trust that by following His will and living a life of faith, we will find true peace and contentment, even in the midst of life's challenges and uncertainties.

So today, let's remember the importance of prayer and trust in finding peace in every situation. Let's make prayer a priority in our lives, seeking God's guidance and wisdom in all aspects of our lives. Let's cultivate a spirit of thanksgiving and focus on the blessings and goodness of God. And let's keep our focus on Christ and His calling for our lives, trusting in His provision and care as we seek to live out His love and grace in the world around us.

DAY 12 Seeking Wisdom: Listening to the Counsel of Others

Proverbs 1:8-9 Updated American Standard Version (UASV)

[8] Hear, my son, your father's instruction,
  and do not forsake your mother's teaching,
[9] for they are a graceful garland for your head
  and pendants for your neck.

Commentary

Proverbs 1:8-9 is a passage that emphasizes the importance of listening to and following the wisdom of parents. In these verses, the author writes, "Listen, my son, to your father's instruction and do not forsake your mother's teaching. They are a garland to grace your head and a chain to adorn your neck."

These verses are particularly relevant in the context of the book of Proverbs, which is a collection of wisdom sayings that emphasize the importance of living a life of righteousness, obedience, and wisdom. The author encourages his readers to listen to the wisdom of their parents and to seek out the guidance and wisdom of others who have gone before them.

This passage also has broader implications for our lives as believers. It reminds us of the importance of seeking out the wisdom and guidance of others, particularly those who have more experience or knowledge than we do. It encourages us to listen carefully to the counsel of others and to apply their wisdom to our lives.

Ultimately, Proverbs 1:8-9 is a powerful reminder of the importance of seeking out the wisdom of others as we navigate the challenges and uncertainties of life. It reminds us that by listening to the guidance and wisdom of those who have gone before us, we can avoid making the same mistakes and pitfalls, and grow in our knowledge and understanding of God's will and purpose for our lives. By seeking out the wisdom of others, we can live a life of righteousness and obedience, and find true fulfillment and joy in the world around us.

Devotional for Youth

As teenagers, we often face many challenges and uncertainties in our lives. We may be struggling with academic or personal challenges or navigating the complexities of relationships and friendships. In the midst of these challenges, it can be easy to feel lost or unsure of which direction to take.

However, in Proverbs 1:8-9, the author reminds us of the importance of seeking out the wisdom and guidance of others, particularly those who have more experience or knowledge than we do. He encourages us to listen to the counsel of our parents, recognizing that their wisdom can help guide us in making wise decisions and avoiding pitfalls.

So how can we seek wisdom and listen to the counsel of others?

Firstly, we can make a commitment to learning from others. We can seek out the guidance and wisdom of parents, mentors, pastors, or friends who have more experience or knowledge than we do. We can ask for their advice and listen carefully to their counsel, recognizing that their wisdom can help us make wise decisions and avoid mistakes.

Secondly, we can cultivate a spirit of humility in our lives. We can recognize that we don't have all the answers and that we need the guidance and wisdom of others to navigate life's challenges. By cultivating a spirit of humility, we can be open to the guidance and counsel of others, and be willing to learn from their wisdom.

Lastly, we can keep our focus on Christ and His calling for our lives. We can seek to use our talents and passions to serve Him and to bring glory to His name. We can trust that by following His will and living a life of wisdom and obedience, we will find true fulfillment and joy in the world around us.

So today, let's remember the importance of seeking wisdom and listening to the counsel of others. Let's make a commitment to learning from those who have gone before us, and to being open to their guidance and advice. Let's cultivate a spirit of humility and recognize that we need the wisdom and guidance of others to navigate life's challenges. And let's keep our focus on Christ and His calling for our lives, trusting in His provision and guidance as we seek to live out His love and grace in the world around us.

DAY 13 Trusting in God: Finding Guidance and Direction

Proverbs 3:5-6 Updated American Standard Version (UASV)

⁵ Trust in Jehovah with all your heart,
    and do not lean on your own understanding.
⁶ In all your ways acknowledge him,
    and he will make straight your paths.

Commentary

Proverbs 3:5-6 is a well-known passage that emphasizes the importance of trust in the lives of believers. In these verses, the author writes, "Trust in Jehovah with all your heart and lean not on your own understanding; in all your ways submit to him, and he will make your paths straight."

These verses are particularly relevant in the context of the book of Proverbs, which emphasizes the importance of wisdom and obedience in navigating the challenges and uncertainties of life. The author encourages his readers to trust in God's provision and guidance, rather than relying on their own understanding or wisdom.

This passage also has broader implications for our lives as believers. It reminds us of the importance of trusting in God's provision and guidance in every aspect of our lives, and submitting our plans and desires to His will. It encourages us to rely on God's wisdom and understanding, rather than our own limited perspective.

Ultimately, Proverbs 3:5-6 is a powerful reminder of the transformative power of trust in our lives as believers. It reminds us that by submitting our plans and desires to God, we can experience His provision and guidance, and find the strength and wisdom we need to navigate life's challenges. By trusting in God's wisdom and understanding, we can live a life of obedience and fulfillment, and find true joy and peace in the world around us.

Devotional for Youth

As teenagers, we often face many challenges and uncertainties in our lives. We may be struggling with academic or personal challenges or navigating the complexities of relationships and friendships. In the midst of these challenges, it can be easy to feel lost or unsure of which direction to take.

However, in Proverbs 3:5-6, the author reminds us of the importance of trust in finding guidance and direction. He encourages us to trust in Jehovah with all our heart, and to submit all our ways to Him. He reminds us that when we do, He will make our paths straight.

So how can we trust in God and find guidance and direction in our lives?

Firstly, we can make a commitment to seek God's guidance in every aspect of our lives. We can make time for prayer, seeking His guidance and wisdom in all our decisions and plans. We can ask for His guidance and direction, trusting that He will provide us with the strength and guidance we need to navigate life's challenges.

Secondly, we can cultivate a spirit of surrender in our lives. We can recognize that our own understanding and wisdom is limited, and that we need to submit our plans and desires to God's will. By surrendering our plans and desires to Him, we can trust that He will provide us with the guidance and direction we need to navigate life's challenges.

Lastly, we can keep our focus on Christ and His calling for our lives. We can seek to use our talents and passions to serve Him and to bring glory to His name. We can trust that by following His will and living a life of obedience, we will find true fulfillment and joy in the world around us.

So today, let's remember the importance of trust in finding guidance and direction. Let's make a commitment to seek God's guidance and wisdom in all aspects of our lives, and to submit our plans and desires to His will. Let's cultivate a spirit of surrender, and trust that He will make our paths straight as we seek to live out His love and grace in the world around us.

DAY 14 Finding Rest in Jesus

Matthew 11:28-30 Updated American Standard Version (UASV)

[28] "Come to me, all you who are laboring and loaded down, and I will give you rest. [29] Take my yoke upon you and learn from me, for I am gentle and lowly in heart, and you will find rest for your souls. [30] For my yoke is easy, and my burden is light."

Commentary

Matthew 11:28-30 is a well-known passage in which Jesus invites all who are weary and burdened to come to Him for rest. He says, "Come to me, all you who are weary and burdened, and I will give you rest. Take my yoke upon you and learn from me, for I am gentle and humble in heart, and you will find rest for your souls. For my yoke is easy and my burden is light."

These verses are particularly relevant in the context of the Gospel of Matthew, which emphasizes Jesus as the Messiah who has come to bring salvation and rest to all who believe in Him. In these verses, Jesus invites all who are weary and burdened to come to Him and find rest for their souls. He assures them that His yoke is easy and His burden is light, and that by learning from Him, they will find the peace and rest they are searching for.

This passage also has broader implications for our lives as believers. It reminds us of the importance of coming to Jesus in times of weariness and burden and finding rest in Him. It encourages us to take on His yoke and learn from Him, recognizing that by following His will and living a life of obedience, we will find true fulfillment and rest.

Ultimately, Matthew 11:28-30 is a powerful reminder of the rest and peace that come from a life lived in faith and trust in Jesus. It reminds us that by coming to Him in times of weariness and burden, and by following His will and living a life of obedience, we can find the rest and peace we are searching for, and experience the transformative power of His love and grace in our lives.

Devotional for Youth

As teenagers, we often face many challenges and uncertainties in our lives. We may be struggling with academic or personal challenges or navigating the complexities of relationships and friendships. In the midst of these challenges, it can be easy to feel weary and burdened, and to wonder if we will ever find rest.

However, in Matthew 11:28-30, Jesus reminds us of the rest and peace that come from a life lived in faith and trust in Him. He invites all who are weary and burdened to come to Him and find rest for their souls. He assures us that His yoke is easy and His burden is light, and that by learning from Him, we will find the peace and rest we are searching for.

So how can we find rest in Jesus?

Firstly, we can make a commitment to come to Him in times of weariness and burden. We can make time for prayer, seeking His guidance and wisdom in all our challenges and struggles. We can ask for His strength and peace, trusting that He will provide us with the rest we need to navigate life's challenges.

Secondly, we can take on Jesus' yoke and learn from Him. We can read His word, seeking to understand His will and His ways. We can seek to imitate His love and compassion, and to live a life of obedience and service to Him. By taking on His yoke and learning from Him, we can find the peace and rest we are searching for.

Lastly, we can keep our focus on Christ and His calling for our lives. We can seek to use our talents and passions to serve Him and to bring glory to His name. We can trust that by following His will and living a life of obedience, we will find true fulfillment and rest in the world around us.

So today, let's remember the rest and peace that come from a life lived in faith and trust in Jesus. Let's make a commitment to come to Him in times of weariness and burden, and to take on His yoke and learn from Him. And let's keep our focus on Him and His calling for our lives, trusting in His provision and guidance as we seek to live out His love and grace in the world around us.

DAY 15 Finding Strength in God

Isaiah 40:29-31 Updated American Standard Version (UASV)

²⁹ He gives power to the tired one,
and full might to those lacking strength.
³⁰ Youths will tire out and grow weary,
And young men will stumble and fall;
³¹ But those hoping in Jehovah will regain power;
they will soar on wings like eagles;
they will run and not grow weary;
they will walk and not tire out.

Commentary

Isaiah 40:29-31 is a powerful passage that speaks to the strength and power that God provides to those who trust in Him. In these verses, the author writes, "He gives strength to the weary and increases the power of the weak. Even youths grow tired and weary, and young men stumble and fall; but those who hope in Jehovah will renew their strength. They will soar on wings like eagles; they will run and not grow weary, they will walk and not be faint."

These verses are particularly relevant in the context of the book of Isaiah, which emphasizes God's sovereignty and power over all creation. In these verses, the author reminds us of God's power to provide strength to the weary and to increase the power of the weak. He assures us that even when we grow tired and weary, God is with us, and will renew our strength when we place our hope and trust in Him.

This passage also has broader implications for our lives as believers. It reminds us of the importance of placing our hope and trust in God, particularly in times of weariness or weakness. It encourages us to rely on His strength and power, rather than our own, recognizing that by doing so, we will find the strength we need to overcome life's challenges and to live a life of obedience and faithfulness.

Ultimately, Isaiah 40:29-31 is a powerful reminder of the strength and power that come from placing our hope and trust in God. It reminds us that by relying on His strength and power, we can find the strength and courage we need to navigate life's challenges, and to live a life of obedience and faithfulness to Him. By placing our hope in Him, we can experience the transformative power of His love and grace in our lives and find true strength and power in the world around us.

Devotional for Youth

As teenagers, we often face many challenges and uncertainties in our lives. We may be struggling with academic or personal challenges or navigating the complexities of relationships and friendships. In the midst of these challenges, it can be easy to feel tired or weak, and to wonder if we have the strength to face the challenges ahead.

However, in Isaiah 40:29-31, the author reminds us of the strength and power that come from placing our hope and trust in God. He reminds us that even when we feel weak or tired, God is with us, and will renew our strength when we place our hope and trust in Him.

So how can we find strength in God?

Firstly, we can make a commitment to place our hope and trust in Him. We can make time for prayer and meditation, seeking His guidance and wisdom in all our challenges and struggles. We can ask for His strength and power, trusting that He will provide us with the strength we need to navigate life's challenges.

Secondly, we can cultivate a spirit of surrender in our lives. We can recognize that our own strength and power is limited, and that we need to rely on God's strength and power to overcome life's challenges. By surrendering our plans and desires to Him, we can trust that He will provide us with the strength we need to navigate life's challenges.

Lastly, we can keep our focus on God and His calling for our lives. We can seek to use our talents and passions to serve Him and to bring glory to His name. We can trust that by following His will and living a life of obedience, we will find true strength and power in the world around us.

So today, let's remember the strength and power that come from placing our hope and trust in God. Let's make a commitment to rely on His strength and power to overcome life's challenges, and to surrender our plans and desires to Him. And let's keep our focus on Him and His calling for our lives, trusting in His provision and guidance as we seek to live out His love and grace in the world around us.

DAY 16 Honoring Parents as a Christian

Ephesians 6:1-3 Updated American Standard Version (UASV)

6 Children, obey your parents in the Lord, for this is right. ² Honor your father and mother (which is the first commandment with a promise), ³ that it may go well with you and that you may live long in the land.

Commentary

Ephesians 6:1-3 is a passage that addresses the importance of honoring parents in the context of a Christian household. The author writes, "Children, obey your parents in the Lord, for this is right. 'Honor your father and mother'—which is the first commandment with a promise— 'so that it may go well with you and that you may enjoy long life on the earth.'"

This passage is particularly relevant in the context of the letter to the Ephesians, which emphasizes the importance of living a life of obedience to God's will. In these verses, the author reminds children of their responsibility to obey and honor their parents, recognizing that this is a crucial aspect of living a life of obedience and faithfulness to God.

This passage also has broader implications for our lives as believers. It reminds us of the importance of respecting and honoring those in authority over us, recognizing that this is an important aspect of living a life of obedience and faithfulness to God. It encourages us to recognize the wisdom and guidance that our parents can provide, and to seek to honor them in all aspects of our lives.

Ultimately, Ephesians 6:1-3 is a powerful reminder of the importance of honoring parents and those in authority over us, recognizing that this is an important aspect of living a life of obedience and faithfulness to God. It reminds us that by honoring those in authority over us, we can experience the transformative power of God's love and grace in our lives and find true joy and fulfillment in the world around us.

Devotional for Youth

As teenagers, we are often seeking greater independence and autonomy in our lives. We may feel that our parents don't understand us or our goals, and that we would be better off making our own decisions. However, in Ephesians 6:1-3, the author reminds us of the importance of honoring parents and those in authority over us, recognizing that this is a crucial aspect of living a life of obedience and faithfulness to God.

So how can we honor our parents as Christians?

Firstly, we can make a commitment to obey our parents in the Lord. We can seek to understand their guidance and wisdom, recognizing that they have our best interests at heart. We can make time to listen to their counsel and advice, seeking to learn from their experiences and insights.

Secondly, we can cultivate a spirit of gratitude in our lives. We can recognize the sacrifices that our parents have made for us, and express our appreciation for all that they do for us. By cultivating a spirit of gratitude, we can deepen our relationship with our parents, and show them the respect and honor that they deserve.

Lastly, we can keep our focus on God and His calling for our lives. We can seek to use our talents and passions to serve Him and to bring glory to His name. We can trust that by following His will and living a life of obedience, we will find true joy and fulfillment in the world around us.

So today, let's remember the importance of honoring our parents as Christians. Let's make a commitment to obey them in the Lord, and to cultivate a spirit of gratitude in our lives. And let's keep our focus on God and His calling for our lives, trusting in His provision and guidance as we seek to live out His love and grace in the world around us.

DAY 17 Overcoming Fear with God's Power

2 Timothy 1:7 Updated American Standard Version (UASV)

[7] For God did not give us a spirit of cowardice, but one of power and of love and of soundness of mind.[2]

Commentary

2 Timothy 1:7 is a powerful and encouraging verse that speaks to the transformative power of God's love and grace in our lives. The author writes, "For God has not given us a spirit of fear and timidity, but of power, love, and self-discipline."

This verse is particularly relevant in the context of Paul's letter to Timothy, which emphasizes the importance of living a life of faith and obedience to God's will. In these verses, the author reminds us that the spirit that God has given us is not one of fear and timidity, but of power, love, and self-discipline. He assures us that by relying on God's strength and power, we can overcome our fears and live a life of courage and boldness.

This verse also has broader implications for our lives as believers. It reminds us that as Christians, we have been given a spirit of power, love, and self-discipline, and that we can rely on God's strength and guidance to overcome our fears and to live a life of faith and obedience. It encourages us to trust in God's provision and guidance, and to seek to live a life of boldness and courage in the world around us.

Ultimately, 2 Timothy 1:7 is a powerful reminder of the transformative power of God's love and grace in our lives. It reminds us that by relying on God's strength and power, we can

---

[2] **Sound in Mind**: (Gr. *sophroneo*) This means to be of sound mind or in one's right mind, i.e., to have understanding about practical matters and thus be able to act sensibly, 'to have sound judgment, to be sensible, to use good sense, sound judgment.' – Acts 26:25; Romans 12:3; 2 Timothy 1:7; Titus 2:6; 1 Peter 4:7.

overcome our fears and live a life of boldness and courage, trusting in His provision and guidance every step of the way.

Devotional for Youth

As teenagers, we often face many fears and uncertainties in our lives. We may be worried about the future, or anxious about our relationships or academic performance. In the midst of these fears, it can be easy to feel overwhelmed and powerless.

However, in 2 Timothy 1:7, the author reminds us of the transformative power of God's love and grace in our lives. He reminds us that the spirit that God has given us is not one of fear and timidity, but of power, love, and self-discipline. He assures us that by relying on God's strength and power, we can overcome our fears and live a life of boldness and courage.

So how can we overcome our fears with God's power?

Firstly, we can make a commitment to trust in God's provision and guidance. We can seek to deepen our relationship with Him through prayer, worship, and Bible study, recognizing that He is always with us, even in the midst of our fears and uncertainties.

Secondly, we can cultivate a spirit of love in our lives. We can seek to love and serve others, recognizing that by doing so, we can overcome our fears and live a life of boldness and courage. By showing love to those around us, we can demonstrate the transformative power of God's love and grace in our lives.

Lastly, we can keep our focus on God and His calling for our lives. We can seek to use our talents and passions to serve Him and to bring glory to His name. We can trust that by following His will and living a life of obedience, we will find true joy and fulfillment in the world around us.

So today, let's remember the transformative power of God's love and grace in our lives. Let's make a commitment to overcome our fears with God's power, and to cultivate a spirit of love and obedience in our lives. And let's keep our focus on God and His calling for our lives, trusting in His provision and guidance as we seek to live out His love and grace in the world around us.

DAY 18 Trusting God in the Present Moment

Matthew 6:34 Updated American Standard Version (UASV)

³⁴ "'Therefore do not be anxious about tomorrow, for tomorrow will be anxious for itself. Sufficient for the day is its own wickedness.

Commentary

Matthew 6:34 is a verse that speaks to the importance of living in the present moment and trusting in God's provision and guidance in our lives. The author writes, "Therefore do not worry about tomorrow, for tomorrow will worry about itself. Each day has enough trouble of its own."

This verse is particularly relevant in the context of Jesus' Sermon on the Mount, which emphasizes the importance of living a life of faith and obedience to God's will. In these verses, the author reminds us that worrying about the future only adds unnecessary stress and anxiety to our lives, and that we can trust in God's provision and guidance to help us navigate life's challenges.

This verse also has broader implications for our lives as believers. It encourages us to live in the present moment, trusting in God's provision and guidance for each day. It reminds us that by focusing on the present moment, and trusting in God's provision and guidance, we can overcome our fears and anxieties, and live a life of faith and obedience.

Ultimately, Matthew 6:34 is a powerful reminder of the importance of living in the present moment, and trusting in God's provision and guidance for each day. It reminds us that by living a life of faith and obedience, and by trusting in God's provision and guidance, we can experience the transformative power of His love and grace in our lives and find true joy and fulfillment in the world around us.

Devotional for Youth

As teenagers, we often worry about the future, and the challenges that lie ahead. We may be worried about our academic performance, or anxious about our relationships or career paths. In the midst of these worries, it can be easy to lose sight of the present moment, and to forget the importance of living in the here and now.

However, in Matthew 6:34, Jesus reminds us of the transformative power of living in the present moment, and trusting in God's provision and guidance for each day. He encourages us not to worry about tomorrow, but to focus on the challenges and opportunities that we face today.

So how can we trust God in the present moment?

Firstly, we can make a commitment to focus on the present moment. We can seek to be fully present in each moment, recognizing the beauty and wonder of the world around us. By focusing on the present moment, we can cultivate a spirit of gratitude and joy, and experience the transformative power of God's love and grace in our lives.

Secondly, we can cultivate a spirit of trust in God's provision and guidance. We can seek to deepen our relationship with Him through prayer, worship, and Bible study, recognizing that He is always with us, even in the midst of life's challenges and uncertainties. By trusting in God's provision and guidance, we can overcome our fears and anxieties, and experience the transformative power of His love and grace in our lives.

Lastly, we can keep our focus on God's calling for our lives. We can seek to use our talents and passions to serve Him and to bring glory to His name. We can trust that by following His will and living a life of obedience, we will find true joy and fulfillment in the world around us.

So today, let's remember the transformative power of living in the present moment, and trusting in God's provision and guidance for each day. Let's make a commitment to focus on the present moment, and to cultivate a spirit of trust and obedience in our lives.

And let's keep our focus on God's calling for our lives, trusting in His provision and guidance as we seek to live out His love and grace in the world around us.

DAY 19 Finding Joy in Trials and Tribulations

James 1:2-4 Updated American Standard Version (UASV)

[2] Consider it all joy, my brothers, when you encounter various trials, [3] knowing that the testing of your faith produces endurance. [4] And let endurance have its perfect work, so that you may be perfect and complete, lacking in nothing.

Commentary

James 1:2-4 is a powerful and encouraging passage that speaks to the transformative power of trials and tribulations in our lives. The author writes, "Consider it pure joy, my brothers and sisters, whenever you face trials of many kinds, because you know that the testing of your faith produces perseverance. Let perseverance finish its work so that you may be mature and complete, not lacking anything."

This passage is particularly relevant in the context of James' letter to the early Christian community, which emphasizes the importance of living a life of faith and obedience to God's will. In these verses, the author reminds us that trials and tribulations are an important part of our spiritual growth and development, and that by persevering through these challenges, we can become mature and complete in our faith.

This passage also has broader implications for our lives as believers. It encourages us to embrace trials and tribulations as opportunities for growth and transformation, recognizing that these challenges can help us to develop perseverance and resilience in our faith. It reminds us that by trusting in God's provision and guidance, and by persevering through life's challenges, we can experience the transformative power of His love and grace in our lives.

Ultimately, James 1:2-4 is a powerful reminder of the importance of persevering through trials and tribulations in our lives. It reminds us that by trusting in God's provision and guidance, and by embracing the challenges that we face, we can experience the transformative power of His love and grace in our lives and become mature and complete in our faith.

Devotional for Youth

As teenagers, we often face many trials and tribulations in our lives. We may be struggling with academic performance or dealing with the challenges of our relationships or mental health. In the midst of these challenges, it can be easy to feel overwhelmed and discouraged.

However, in James 1:2-4, the author reminds us of the transformative power of trials and tribulations in our lives. He encourages us to consider it pure joy whenever we face trials of many kinds, recognizing that these challenges can help us to develop perseverance and resilience in our faith.

So how can we find joy in trials and tribulations?

Firstly, we can make a commitment to trust in God's provision and guidance. We can seek to deepen our relationship with Him through prayer, worship, and Bible study, recognizing that He is always with us, even in the midst of life's challenges and uncertainties. By trusting in God's provision and guidance, we can experience the transformative power of His love and grace in our lives, and find joy and peace in the midst of our trials.

Secondly, we can cultivate a spirit of perseverance in our faith. We can seek to develop resilience and strength in the face of life's challenges, recognizing that these trials can help us to become mature and complete in our faith. By persevering through our trials and tribulations, we can experience the transformative power of God's love and grace in our lives and become the people that He has called us to be.

Lastly, we can keep our focus on God's calling for our lives. We can seek to use our talents and passions to serve Him and to bring glory to His name, even in the midst of our trials and tribulations. By keeping our focus on God's will and living a life of obedience, we can experience the transformative power of His love and grace in our lives and find true joy and fulfillment in the world around us.

So today, let's remember the transformative power of trials and tribulations in our lives. Let's make a commitment to trust in God's provision and guidance, to cultivate a spirit of perseverance in our faith, and to keep our focus on God's calling for our lives. And let's find joy and peace in the midst of our trials, recognizing that by trusting in God's provision and guidance, we can experience the transformative power of His love and grace in our lives.

DAY 20 Finding Comfort in God's Presence

Psalm 23:4 Updated American Standard Version (UASV)

⁴ Even though I walk through the valley of the shadow of death,
    I will fear no evil,
for you are with me;
    your rod and your staff,
    they comfort me.

Commentary

Psalm 23:4 is one of the most beloved and comforting passages in the Bible. The author writes, "Even though I walk through the darkest valley, I will fear no evil, for you are with me; your rod and your staff, they comfort me."

This passage speaks to the transformative power of God's presence and guidance in our lives, even in the midst of life's greatest challenges and uncertainties. It reminds us that by trusting in God's provision and guidance, we can overcome our fears and anxieties, and experience the transformative power of His love and grace in our lives.

This passage is particularly relevant in the context of the psalmist's life, which was filled with many challenges and uncertainties. It reminds us that even in the midst of life's darkest moments, God is with us, and that we can find comfort and peace in His presence.

Ultimately, Psalm 23:4 is a powerful reminder of the importance of trusting in God's provision and guidance, and of finding comfort and peace in His presence. It reminds us that by keeping our focus on Him, even in the midst of life's greatest challenges, we can experience the transformative power of His love and grace in our lives.

Devotional for Youth

As teenagers, we often face many challenges and uncertainties in our lives. We may be struggling with academic performance or dealing with the challenges of our relationships or mental health. In the midst of these challenges, it can be easy to feel overwhelmed and discouraged.

However, in Psalm 23:4, the author reminds us of the transformative power of God's presence and guidance in our lives. He encourages us to find comfort and peace in the midst of life's greatest challenges, recognizing that even in the darkest valleys, God is with us.

So how can we find comfort in God's presence?

Firstly, we can make a commitment to trust in God's provision and guidance. We can seek to deepen our relationship with Him through prayer, worship, and Bible study, recognizing that He is always with us, even in the midst of life's challenges and uncertainties. By trusting in God's provision and guidance, we can experience the transformative power of His love and grace in our lives and find comfort and peace in His presence.

Secondly, we can cultivate a spirit of gratitude in our lives. We can seek to recognize the many blessings that God has given us, even in the midst of life's challenges and uncertainties. By cultivating a spirit of gratitude, we can experience the transformative power of God's love and grace in our lives and find comfort and peace in His presence.

Lastly, we can keep our focus on God's will and purpose for our lives. We can seek to use our talents and passions to serve Him and to bring glory to His name, even in the midst of our challenges and uncertainties. By keeping our focus on God's will and living a life of obedience, we can experience the transformative power of His love and grace in our lives and find true joy and fulfillment in the world around us.

So today, let's remember the transformative power of God's presence and guidance in our lives. Let's make a commitment to trust in His provision and guidance, to cultivate a spirit of gratitude, and to keep our focus on His will and purpose for our lives. And let's find comfort and peace in His presence, recognizing that even in the darkest valleys, He is with us, guiding us and comforting us with His love and grace.

DAY 21 Trusting in God's Provision

Psalm 34:10 Updated American Standard Version (UASV)

¹⁰ The young lions do lack and suffer hunger;
but those who seek Jehovah lack no good thing.

Commentary

Psalm 34:10 is a powerful and encouraging passage that speaks to the abundance of God's provision in our lives. The author writes, "The lions may grow weak and hungry, but those who seek Jehovah lack no good thing."

This passage reminds us that when we seek God and trust in His provision, we will lack no good thing. It speaks to the transformative power of God's love and grace in our lives, and encourages us to place our trust in Him, even in the midst of life's greatest challenges and uncertainties.

This passage also has broader implications for our lives as believers. It encourages us to seek God and His will above all else, recognizing that by doing so, we will experience the abundance of His provision and grace in our lives. It reminds us that by trusting in His guidance and provision, we can overcome our fears and anxieties, and experience the transformative power of His love and grace in our lives.

Ultimately, Psalm 34:10 is a powerful reminder of the importance of seeking God's provision and guidance in our lives, and of the transformative power of His love and grace. It reminds us that by keeping our focus on Him and trusting in His provision, we can experience the abundance of His blessings and live a life of true joy and fulfillment.

Devotional for Youth

As teenagers, we often face many challenges and uncertainties in our lives. We may be struggling with academic performance or dealing with the challenges of our relationships or mental health. In the midst of these challenges, it can be easy to feel overwhelmed and discouraged.

However, in Psalm 34:10, the author reminds us of the abundance of God's provision in our lives. He encourages us to seek God and His will above all else, recognizing that by doing so, we will lack no good thing.

So how can we trust in God's provision?

Firstly, we can make a commitment to seek God and His will above all else. We can seek to deepen our relationship with Him through prayer, worship, and Bible study, recognizing that He is the source of all good things in our lives. By seeking God and His will, we can experience the transformative power of His love and grace in our lives, and trust in His provision for us.

Secondly, we can cultivate a spirit of gratitude in our lives. We can seek to recognize the many blessings that God has given us, even in the midst of life's challenges and uncertainties. By cultivating a spirit of gratitude, we can experience the abundance of God's provision in our lives, and trust in His goodness and faithfulness.

Lastly, we can keep our focus on God's will and purpose for our lives. We can seek to use our talents and passions to serve Him and to bring glory to His name, recognizing that by doing so, we will experience the abundance of His blessings and provision. By keeping our focus on God's will and living a life of obedience, we can trust in His provision and experience the transformative power of His love and grace in our lives.

So today, let's trust in God's provision for our lives. Let's make a commitment to seek Him and His will above all else, to cultivate a spirit of gratitude, and to keep our focus on His purpose for our lives. And let's trust in His goodness and faithfulness, recognizing that by doing so, we will lack no good thing, and will experience the abundance of His blessings and provision.

DAY 22 Casting Your Cares on God

Psalm 55:22 Updated American Standard Version (UASV)

²² Cast your burden on Jehovah,
    and he will sustain you;
he will never permit
    the righteous to be shaken.

Commentary

Psalm 55:22 is a powerful and encouraging passage that speaks to the transformative power of God's love and protection in our lives. The author writes, "Cast your cares on Jehovah and he will sustain you; he will never let the righteous be shaken."

This passage reminds us that when we cast our cares and burdens on God, He will sustain us and protect us from harm. It speaks to the transformative power of God's love and grace in our lives, and encourages us to place our trust in Him, even in the midst of life's greatest challenges and uncertainties.

This passage also has broader implications for our lives as believers. It encourages us to seek God and His will above all else, recognizing that by doing so, we will experience the transformative power of His love and grace in our lives. It reminds us that by trusting in His guidance and protection, we can overcome our fears and anxieties, and experience the peace and joy that comes from living in His presence.

Ultimately, Psalm 55:22 is a powerful reminder of the importance of trusting in God's protection and care in our lives, and of the transformative power of His love and grace. It reminds us that by keeping our focus on Him and trusting in His provision, we can experience the peace, joy, and fulfillment that comes from living in His presence.

Devotional for Youth

As teenagers, we often face many challenges and uncertainties in our lives. We may be struggling with academic performance, or dealing with the challenges of our relationships or mental health. In the midst of these challenges, it can be easy to feel overwhelmed and burdened.

However, in Psalm 55:22, the author reminds us of the transformative power of God's love and protection in our lives. He encourages us to cast our cares and burdens on God, recognizing that He will sustain us and protect us from harm.

So how can we cast our cares on God?

Firstly, we can make a commitment to seek God and His will above all else. We can seek to deepen our relationship with Him through prayer, worship, and Bible study, recognizing that He is the source of all comfort and strength in our lives. By seeking God and His will, we can experience the transformative power of His love and grace in our lives, and trust in His provision and protection.

Secondly, we can cultivate a spirit of surrender in our lives. We can seek to relinquish control over our circumstances and trust in God's plan and purpose for our lives. By surrendering our cares and burdens to Him, we can experience the peace and joy that comes from living in His presence.

Lastly, we can keep our focus on God's promises and faithfulness. We can seek to meditate on His word and reflect on His goodness and faithfulness in our lives. By keeping our focus on God's promises, we can trust in His provision and protection, even in the midst of life's greatest challenges and uncertainties.

So today, let's cast our cares on God. Let's make a commitment to seek Him and His will above all else, to cultivate a spirit of surrender, and to keep our focus on His promises and faithfulness. And let's trust in His provision and protection, recognizing that He will sustain us and never let us be shaken, and that we can find comfort, strength, and peace in His loving embrace.

DAY 23 The Mighty Warrior Who Delights in Us

Zephaniah 3:17 Updated American Standard Version (UASV)

¹⁷ Jehovah your God is in your midst,
   a mighty one who will save;
he will exult over you with great joy;
   he will quiet you in his love;
he will rejoice over you with shouts of joy.

Commentary

Zephaniah 3:17 is a beautiful and uplifting passage that speaks to the depths of God's love and care for His people. The author writes, "Jehovah your God is with you, the Mighty Warrior who saves. He will take great delight in you; in his love he will no longer rebuke you but will rejoice over you with singing."

This passage reminds us of God's presence and protection in our lives. It speaks to the transformative power of His love and grace and encourages us to trust in His provision and care. It reminds us that no matter what challenges we may face in life, we can always turn to God for strength and comfort.

This passage also has broader implications for our lives as believers. It reminds us that we are deeply loved and cherished by God, and that He delights in us and rejoices over us with singing. It encourages us to live in the fullness of His love and grace, and to seek His will and purpose for our lives.

Ultimately, Zephaniah 3:17 is a powerful reminder of the depths of God's love and care for His people. It reminds us that we are never alone, and that God is always with us, fighting for us and rejoicing over us with singing. It encourages us to trust in His provision and care, and to live in the fullness of His love and grace.

Devotional for Youth

As teenagers, we often face many challenges and uncertainties in our lives. We may be struggling with academic performance, or dealing with the challenges of our relationships or mental health. In the midst of these challenges, it can be easy to feel alone and discouraged.

However, in Zephaniah 3:17, the author reminds us of the depths of God's love and care for His people. He encourages us to trust in God's presence and protection in our lives, and to remember that He is a mighty warrior who saves and delights in us.

So how can we trust in God's love and care?

Firstly, we can make a commitment to seek God and His will above all else. We can seek to deepen our relationship with Him through prayer, worship, and Bible study, recognizing that He is the source of all strength and comfort in our lives. By seeking God and His will, we can experience the transformative power of His love and grace in our lives, and trust in His provision and care.

Secondly, we can cultivate a spirit of gratitude in our lives. We can seek to recognize the many blessings that God has given us, even in the midst of life's challenges and uncertainties. By cultivating a spirit of gratitude, we can experience the joy and peace that comes from living in the fullness of God's love.

Lastly, we can keep our focus on God's promises and faithfulness. We can seek to meditate on His word and reflect on His goodness and faithfulness in our lives. By keeping our focus on God's promises, we can trust in His provision and care, even in the midst of life's greatest challenges and uncertainties.

So today, let's trust in God's love and care for us. Let's make a commitment to seek Him and His will above all else, to cultivate a spirit of gratitude, and to keep our focus on His promises and faithfulness. And let's remember that we are deeply loved and cherished by God, and that He is a mighty warrior who saves and rejoices over us with singing.

DAY 24 Seeking Shrewdness, Knowledge and Thinking Ability

Proverbs 1:4 Updated American Standard Version (UASV)

[4] to give shrewdness[3] to the inexperienced,
  to the young man knowledge[4] and thinking ability.[5]

Commentary

Proverbs 1:4 is a powerful and insightful passage that speaks to the importance of wisdom and understanding in our lives. The author writes, "To give prudence to the simple, knowledge and discretion to the young."

This passage reminds us of the transformative power of wisdom and understanding in our lives. It speaks to the importance of seeking knowledge and discretion, and of cultivating a spirit of wisdom and discernment in our lives. It encourages us to seek the guidance and wisdom of others who are wiser and more experienced than us, and to seek to learn from their example and counsel.

This passage also has broader implications for our lives as believers. It reminds us of the importance of seeking God and His wisdom above all else, and of cultivating a spirit of humility and teachability in our lives. It encourages us to seek the guidance of the Holy Spirit in our lives, and to trust in His guidance and

---

[3] **Shrewdness; prudence; discernment:** (עָרוּם arum) This is one who has or shows good powers of judgment. This one is cautious as he careful to avoid potential problems or dangers, as he desires to avoid potential problems.

[4] **Knowledge** (דַּעַת daath) is the possession of information learned by personal experience, observation, or study. It includes wisdom, understanding, insight, and the ability to live successfully and apply what has been taken into one's heart and mind. The Bible strongly urges us to seek and treasure accurate knowledge, as it is far superior to gold. – Prov. 8:10; 20:15.

[5] **Thinking Ability:** (מְזִמָּה mezimmah) In the evil sense, this can mean wicked plans, evil ideas, schemes, and devices. In the favorable sense, it can mean shrewdness, perceptiveness, discretion, and prudence. In the favorable sense, it is the ability to judge wisely and objectively. *Mezimmah*, therefore, the human mind and thoughts can be used for an admirable and upright end, or for evil purposes. – Ps 10:2; Pro. 1:4; 2:10-12; 5:1-2.

direction as we seek to live in accordance with His will and purpose.

Ultimately, Proverbs 1:4 is a powerful reminder of the importance of wisdom and understanding in our lives. It reminds us that by seeking knowledge and discretion, and by cultivating a spirit of wisdom and discernment, we can experience the transformative power of God's love and grace in our lives and can live in the fullness of His will and purpose for us.

Devotional for Youth

As teenagers, we often face many challenges and uncertainties in our lives. We may be struggling to make decisions about our future, or dealing with the challenges of our relationships or mental health. In the midst of these challenges, it can be easy to feel lost or uncertain.

However, in Proverbs 1:4, the author reminds us of the importance of seeking wisdom and understanding in our lives. He encourages us to seek knowledge and discretion, and to cultivate a spirit of wisdom and discernment.

So how can we seek wisdom and understanding?

Firstly, we can make a commitment to seek God and His will above all else. We can seek to deepen our relationship with Him through prayer, worship, and Bible study, recognizing that He is the source of all wisdom and understanding. By seeking God and His will, we can experience the transformative power of His love and grace in our lives, and gain the wisdom and discernment we need to make wise decisions.

Secondly, we can seek the guidance and wisdom of others who are wiser and more experienced than us. We can seek out mentors and role models who can guide us and provide us with counsel and advice. By seeking the guidance of others, we can gain new insights and perspectives, and make better decisions.

Lastly, we can cultivate a spirit of humility and teachability in our lives. We can recognize that we don't have all the answers, and that there is always more to learn. By cultivating a spirit of humility and teachability, we can learn from our mistakes, and grow in wisdom and understanding.

So today, let's seek wisdom and understanding. Let's make a commitment to seek God and His will above all else, to seek the guidance and wisdom of others, and to cultivate a spirit of humility and teachability in our lives. And let's trust in God's provision and care, recognizing that He is the source of all wisdom and understanding, and that by seeking Him, we can experience the transformative power of His love and grace in our lives.

DAY 25 Soaring on Eagle's Wings

Isaiah 40:31 Updated American Standard Version (UASV)

³¹ But those hoping in Jehovah will regain power;
    they will soar on wings like eagles;
they will run and not grow weary;
    they will walk and not tire out.

Commentary

Isaiah 40:31 is a powerful and inspiring passage that speaks to the strength and perseverance that we can find in God. The author writes, "But those who hope in Jehovah will renew their strength. They will soar on wings like eagles; they will run and not grow weary; they will walk and not be faint."

This passage reminds us of the transformative power of hope and trust in God. It speaks to the strength and perseverance that we can find in Him and encourages us to trust in His provision and care. It reminds us that no matter what challenges we may face in life, we can always turn to God for strength and comfort.

This passage also has broader implications for our lives as believers. It reminds us of the importance of hope and trust in God, and of cultivating a spirit of perseverance and endurance in our lives. It encourages us to seek His will and purpose for our lives, and to trust in His guidance and direction as we seek to live in accordance with His plan.

Ultimately, Isaiah 40:31 is a powerful reminder of the strength and perseverance that we can find in God. It reminds us that by placing our hope and trust in Him, we can soar on wings like eagles, and run and not grow weary. It encourages us to trust in His provision and care, and to live in the fullness of His will and purpose for us.

Devotional for Youth

As teenagers, we often face many challenges and uncertainties in our lives. We may be struggling with academic performance, or dealing with the challenges of our relationships or mental health. In the midst of these challenges, it can be easy to feel discouraged and overwhelmed.

However, in Isaiah 40:31, the author reminds us of the transformative power of hope and trust in God. He encourages us to place our hope in the Lord, and reminds us that by doing so, we can renew our strength and soar on wings like eagles.

So how can we place our hope in God and renew our strength?

Firstly, we can make a commitment to seek God and His will above all else. We can seek to deepen our relationship with Him through prayer, worship, and Bible study, recognizing that He is the source of all strength and comfort in our lives. By seeking God and His will, we can experience the transformative power of His love and grace in our lives and renew our strength.

Secondly, we can cultivate a spirit of perseverance and endurance in our lives. We can recognize that challenges and setbacks are a natural part of life, but that by trusting in God, we can overcome them. By cultivating a spirit of perseverance and endurance, we can run and not grow weary, and walk and not be faint.

Lastly, we can trust in God's provision and care. We can recognize that He is always with us, fighting for us and providing for us. By trusting in His provision and care, we can soar on wings like eagles, and live in the fullness of His will and purpose for us.

So today, let's place our hope in God and renew our strength. Let's make a commitment to seek Him and His will above all else, to cultivate a spirit of perseverance and endurance, and to trust in His provision and care. And let's remember that we can always turn to God for strength and comfort, and that by doing so, we can soar on wings like eagles.

DAY 26 Meditate on God's Word

Joshua 1:8-9 Updated American Standard Version (UASV)

[8] This Book of the Law shall not depart from your mouth, but you shall meditate on it day and night, so that you may be careful to do according to all that is written in it; for then you will make your way prosperous, and then you will have good success. [9] Have I not commanded you? Be strong and courageous! Do not be afraid, and do not be dismayed, for Jehovah your God is with you wherever you go."

Commentary

Joshua 1:8-9 is a powerful and encouraging passage that speaks to the importance of obedience and trust in God. The author writes, "Keep this Book of the Law always on your lips; meditate on it day and night, so that you may be careful to do everything written in it. Then you will be prosperous and successful. Have I not commanded you? Be strong and courageous. Do not be afraid; do not be discouraged, for the Lord your God will be with you wherever you go."

This passage reminds us of the importance of obedience to God's word and of meditating on His promises. It speaks to the transformative power of God's word in our lives and encourages us to trust in Him for guidance and direction. It reminds us that when we are faithful in obedience to God's word, we can experience prosperity and success.

This passage also has broader implications for our lives as believers. It reminds us of the importance of trust and courage in the face of challenges, and of relying on God's presence and guidance in all situations. It encourages us to seek His will and direction in our lives, and to trust in His provision and care.

Ultimately, Joshua 1:8-9 is a powerful reminder of the importance of obedience and trust in God. It reminds us that by meditating on His promises and being faithful in obedience to His word, we can experience His transformative power in our lives. It encourages us to trust in Him for guidance and direction, and to rely on His provision and care as we seek to live in accordance with His will and purpose.

Devotional for Youth

As teenagers, we often face many challenges and uncertainties in our lives. We may be struggling with the pressures of school, or dealing with the challenges of our relationships or mental health. In the midst of these challenges, it can be easy to feel lost or uncertain.

However, in Joshua 1:8-9, the author reminds us of the importance of meditating on God's word and seeking His will for our lives. He encourages us to keep His word on our lips, and to meditate on it day and night, so that we may be careful to do everything written in it. By doing so, we can experience prosperity and success, and be strong and courageous in the face of challenges.

So how can we meditate on God's word and seek His will for our lives?

Firstly, we can make a commitment to prioritize our relationship with God. We can seek to deepen our relationship with Him through prayer, worship, and Bible study, recognizing that His word is a source of strength and comfort in our lives. By prioritizing our relationship with God, we can cultivate a spirit of obedience and trust in Him.

Secondly, we can commit to meditating on His word day and night. We can read the Bible daily and reflect on what it means for our lives. We can memorize key verses and recite them to ourselves throughout the day, reminding ourselves of God's promises and provision in our lives.

Lastly, we can trust in God's presence and guidance in all situations. We can recognize that He is with us wherever we go, and that He will never leave us nor forsake us. By trusting in His presence and guidance, we can be strong and courageous in the face of challenges, knowing that He is with us every step of the way.

So today, let's meditate on God's word and seek His will for our lives. Let's make a commitment to prioritize our relationship with Him, to meditate on His word day and night, and to trust in His presence and guidance in all situations. And let's remember that by seeking God and His will for our lives, we can experience prosperity and success, and be strong and courageous in the face of challenges.

DAY 27 Speak Words of Life

Proverbs 10:11 Updated American Standard Version (UASV)

¹¹ The mouth of the righteous is a fountain of life,
  but the mouth of the wicked conceals violence.

Commentary

Proverbs 10:11 is a simple and powerful proverb that speaks to the importance of our words and the impact they have on others. The author writes, "The mouth of the righteous is a fountain of life, but the mouth of the wicked conceals violence."

This proverb reminds us that the words we speak have the power to either bring life and encouragement, or to cause harm and destruction. It speaks to the importance of using our words wisely, and of recognizing the impact they can have on others.

This proverb also has broader implications for our lives as believers. It reminds us of the importance of living a righteous life, and of being mindful of the impact our words and actions have on those around us. It encourages us to seek God's guidance in our speech and actions, and to strive to bring life and encouragement to those around us.

Ultimately, Proverbs 10:11 is a powerful reminder of the impact our words can have on others. It reminds us that by speaking words of life and encouragement, we can make a positive impact on those around us and bring glory to God. It encourages us to live a righteous life, and to seek God's guidance in all that we say and do.

Devotional for Youth

As teenagers, we often face many challenges and uncertainties in our lives. We may be dealing with the pressures of school, or struggling with relationships and mental health. In the midst of these challenges, it can be easy to become overwhelmed and discouraged.

However, Proverbs 10:11 reminds us of the transformative power of our words and encourages us to speak words of life and encouragement to those around us. The author writes that the mouth of the righteous is a fountain of life, bringing refreshment and encouragement to those who hear it.

So how can we speak words of life and encouragement to those around us?

Firstly, we can be mindful of our speech and the impact it can have on others. We can choose to speak words of kindness and encouragement, and to avoid negative or hurtful words that can cause harm and destruction.

Secondly, we can look for opportunities to build up those around us. We can seek to encourage our friends and family, and to speak life into their situations. We can offer words of support and affirmation and remind them of God's love and provision in their lives.

Lastly, we can make a commitment to seek God's guidance in our speech and actions. We can ask Him to guide us in our interactions with others, and to give us the words to speak in every situation. By seeking God's guidance, we can be confident that the words we speak will bring life and encouragement to those around us.

So today, let's choose to speak words of life and encouragement to those around us. Let's be mindful of the impact our words can have on others and seek to build up those around us with our speech. And let's make a commitment to seek God's guidance in all that we say and do, trusting that He will guide us in speaking words that bring life and encouragement to those around us.

DAY 28 Walking in the Light of God's Truth

Proverbs 4:18-19 Updated American Standard Version (UASV)

¹⁸ But the path of the righteous is like the light of dawn,
   which shines brighter and brighter until full day.
¹⁹ The way of the wicked is like deep darkness;
   they do not know over what they stumble.

Commentary

Proverbs 4:18-19 is a beautiful and encouraging passage that speaks to the importance of walking in the light of God's truth. The author writes, "The path of the righteous is like the morning sun, shining ever brighter till the full light of day. But the way of the wicked is like deep darkness; they do not know what makes them stumble."

This passage reminds us that as believers, our lives should be marked by a continual growth in righteousness and a deepening understanding of God's truth. It speaks to the importance of walking in the light of His truth, and of continually seeking His guidance and direction for our lives.

This passage also has broader implications for our lives as believers. It reminds us that as we walk in the light of God's truth, we can experience a greater sense of clarity and purpose in our lives. It encourages us to seek God's guidance and direction in all that we do, and to trust in His provision and care.

Ultimately, Proverbs 4:18-19 is a powerful reminder of the importance of walking in the light of God's truth. It reminds us that as we seek His guidance and direction, we can experience a greater sense of purpose and clarity in our lives. It encourages us to trust in His provision and care, and to walk in the path of righteousness, ever shining brighter until the full light of day.

Devotional for Youth

As teenagers, we often face many challenges and uncertainties in our lives. We may be struggling with the pressures of school, or dealing with difficult relationships or mental health issues. In the midst of these challenges, it can be easy to feel lost or uncertain about the path we should take.

However, Proverbs 4:18-19 reminds us of the importance of walking in the light of God's truth, and of seeking His guidance and direction for our lives. The author writes that the path of the righteous is like the morning sun, shining ever brighter until the full light of day. This image speaks to the idea of growth and continual progression in our relationship with God.

So how can we walk in the light of God's truth and seek His guidance for our lives?

Firstly, we can prioritize our relationship with God. We can seek to deepen our understanding of His word and His will for our lives, and to develop a close and personal relationship with Him through prayer and worship.

Secondly, we can seek God's guidance and direction in all that we do. We can ask Him to show us the path we should take, and to guide us in making decisions that honor Him and further His kingdom.

Lastly, we can trust in God's provision and care for our lives. We can have faith that as we walk in His truth and seek His guidance, He will provide for our needs and lead us in the path of righteousness.

So today, let's make a commitment to walk in the light of God's truth and seek His guidance and direction for our lives. Let's prioritize our relationship with Him, seek His guidance in all that we do, and trust in His provision and care. And as we do so, may we experience a greater sense of purpose and clarity in our lives, shining ever brighter until the full light of day.

.

Edward D. Andrews

DAY 29 The Power of Our Words

Proverbs 12:18 Updated American Standard Version (UASV)

¹⁸ There is one whose rash words are like sword thrusts,
  but the tongue of the wise brings healing.

Commentary

Proverbs 12:18 is a simple yet profound proverb that speaks to the power of our words. The author writes, "The words of the reckless pierce like swords, but the tongue of the wise brings healing."

This proverb reminds us that our words have the power to either bring harm or healing to those around us. It speaks to the importance of using our words wisely and of being mindful of their impact on others.

This proverb also has broader implications for our lives as believers. It reminds us of the importance of seeking God's guidance in our speech and of being mindful of the impact our words can have on those around us. It encourages us to strive to bring healing and encouragement to those we interact with, rather than causing harm or destruction.

Ultimately, Proverbs 12:18 is a powerful reminder of the impact our words can have on others. It reminds us of the importance of using our words wisely and of being mindful of their impact on those around us. It encourages us to seek God's guidance in our speech and actions, and to strive to bring healing and encouragement to those we interact with.

Devotional for Youth

As teenagers, we often face situations where our words can have a powerful impact on those around us. We may be dealing with conflicts in our relationships, or struggling to communicate with our family or friends. In the midst of these challenges, it can be easy to forget the impact our words can have on others.

However, Proverbs 12:18 reminds us of the power of our words and the importance of using them wisely. The author writes that the words of the reckless can pierce like swords, causing harm and destruction to those around us. On the other hand, the tongue of the wise brings healing and encouragement to those who hear it.

So how can we use our words wisely and bring healing to those around us?

Firstly, we can be mindful of the impact our words can have on others. We can choose to speak words of kindness and encouragement, rather than negative or hurtful words that can cause harm and destruction.

Secondly, we can look for opportunities to build up those around us. We can seek to encourage our friends and family, and to speak life into their situations. We can offer words of support and affirmation and remind them of God's love and provision in their lives.

Lastly, we can make a commitment to seek God's guidance in our speech and actions. We can ask Him to guide us in our interactions with others, and to give us the words to speak in every situation. By seeking God's guidance, we can be confident that the words we speak will bring healing and encouragement to those around us.

So today, let's choose to use our words wisely and bring healing and encouragement to those around us. Let's be mindful of the impact our words can have on others and seek to build up those around us with our speech. And let's make a commitment to seek God's guidance in all that we say and do, trusting that He will guide us in speaking words that bring healing and encouragement to those around us.

DAY 30 Seeking Wisdom and Understanding

Proverbs 9:4-6 Updated American Standard Version (UASV)

⁴ "Whoever is simple,⁶ let him turn in here!"
As for him who is in want of heart,⁷ she says to him,
⁵ "Come, eat of my bread
and drink of the wine I have mixed.
⁶ Leave your simple ways,⁸ and live,
and walk in the way of understanding."

Commentary

Proverbs 9:4-6 is a beautiful and powerful passage that speaks to the importance of seeking wisdom and understanding. The author writes, "Let all who are simple come to my house!" To those who have no sense she says, "Come, eat my food and drink the wine I have mixed. Leave your simple ways and you will live; walk in the way of insight."

This passage reminds us that wisdom and understanding are essential for living a fulfilling and purposeful life. It speaks to the importance of seeking out wisdom and guidance from those who are wiser than ourselves, and of being willing to learn and grow in our understanding of God's truth.

This passage also has broader implications for our lives as believers. It reminds us of the importance of seeking out mentors and spiritual leaders who can guide us in our faith, and of being willing to learn from those who are wiser and more experienced than ourselves.

---

⁶ That is, *inexperienced.*

⁷ That is, *lacking good sense.*

⁸ That is *inexperience.*

Ultimately, Proverbs 9:4-6 is a powerful reminder of the importance of seeking wisdom and understanding in our lives. It encourages us to be open to learning and growth, and to seek out guidance and mentorship from those who can help us grow in our understanding of God's truth.

Devotional for Youth

As teenagers, we often face situations where we may feel unsure or inexperienced. We may be navigating new relationships, facing difficult decisions, or trying to understand our place in the world. In the midst of these challenges, it can be easy to feel lost or uncertain about the path we should take.

However, Proverbs 9:4-6 reminds us of the importance of seeking wisdom and understanding in our lives. The author writes that those who are simple should come to the house of wisdom and partake of her food and wine. By doing so, they can leave their simple ways and walk in the way of insight, experiencing life to the fullest.

So how can we seek wisdom and understanding in our lives?

Firstly, we can seek out mentors and spiritual leaders who can guide us in our faith. We can look for those who are wiser and more experienced than ourselves and ask them to share their wisdom and insight with us.

Secondly, we can prioritize our relationship with God and seek to deepen our understanding of His word and His will for our lives. We can spend time in prayer and reflection, asking God to guide us in our decisions and to give us the wisdom and insight we need to navigate life's challenges.

Lastly, we can be open to learning and growth, and be willing to admit when we don't know everything. We can seek out opportunities to learn from others and be willing to ask questions and seek out guidance when we need it.

So today, let's make a commitment to seek wisdom and understanding in our lives. Let's look for mentors and spiritual leaders who can guide us in our faith, prioritize our relationship with God, and be open to learning and growth. And as we do so, may we experience the fullness of life that comes from walking in the way of insight and understanding.

DAY 31 Guarding Your Heart

Proverbs 4:23 Updated American Standard Version (UASV)

²³ Keep your heart with all vigilance,
for from it flow the springs of life.

Commentary

Proverbs 4:23 is a powerful proverb that speaks to the importance of guarding our hearts. The author writes, "Above all else, guard your heart, for everything you do flows from it."

This proverb reminds us that our hearts are the source of everything we do. It speaks to the importance of being mindful of the things we allow into our hearts and minds, and of being intentional about the things we focus on and prioritize in our lives.

This proverb also has broader implications for our lives as believers. It reminds us of the importance of seeking God's guidance in all that we do, and of being mindful of the impact our choices and actions can have on our spiritual well-being. It encourages us to guard our hearts against things that can lead us away from God and His truth, and to prioritize our relationship with Him above all else.

Ultimately, Proverbs 4:23 is a powerful reminder of the importance of guarding our hearts and minds in all that we do. It encourages us to seek God's guidance in all that we do, and to prioritize our relationship with Him above all else. By doing so, we can live lives that are pleasing to Him and that reflect His love and truth to those around us.

Devotional for Youth

As teenagers, we face a world filled with distractions and temptations. We are bombarded with messages from social media, television, and our peers, and it can be easy to get caught up in the things that the world tells us are important. In the midst of all this, it can be easy to forget the importance of guarding our hearts and minds.

Proverbs 4:23 reminds us of the importance of guarding our hearts above all else. The author writes that everything we do flows from our hearts, and that it is essential to be mindful of the things we allow into our hearts and minds.

So how can we guard our hearts and minds in a world that is constantly vying for our attention?

Firstly, we can prioritize our relationship with God and seek to align our hearts and minds with His truth. We can spend time in prayer and reflection, asking God to reveal His truth to us and to help us discern what is good and true in a world that is often confusing and chaotic.

Secondly, we can be intentional about the things we focus on and prioritize in our lives. We can seek out positive influences, surround ourselves with people who encourage and support us, and make choices that align with our values and beliefs.

Lastly, we can be mindful of the impact our choices and actions can have on our spiritual well-being. We can seek to avoid things that can lead us away from God and His truth and be intentional about the things we allow into our hearts and minds.

So today, let's make a commitment to guard our hearts and minds. Let's prioritize our relationship with God, seek out positive influences, and be mindful of the impact our choices and actions can have on our spiritual well-being. And as we do so, may we experience the fullness of life that comes from living in alignment with God's truth and love.

DAY 32 Being a Wise and Discerning Friend

Proverbs 27:11 Updated American Standard Version (UASV)

¹¹ Be wise, my son, and make my heart glad,
    that I may return a word to my reproacher.⁹

Commentary

Proverbs 27:11 is a proverb that speaks to the importance of being a wise and discerning friend. The author writes, "Be wise, my son, and bring joy to my heart; then I can answer anyone who treats me with contempt."

This proverb reminds us of the importance of being a good friend to those around us. It speaks to the power of friendship to bring joy and fulfillment to our lives, and of the importance of being a wise and discerning friend who can provide guidance and support to those who need it.

At the same time, this proverb also reminds us of the importance of being mindful of the impact our friendships can have on others. It encourages us to be wise and discerning in our relationships, and to be willing to stand up for our friends in the face of criticism or contempt.

Ultimately, Proverbs 27:11 is a powerful reminder of the importance of being a wise and discerning friend. It encourages us to seek out friendships that bring joy and fulfillment to our lives, and to be willing to provide guidance and support to those who need it. And as we do so, may we bring joy to the hearts of those around us and stand up for our friends in the face of adversity.

Devotional for Youth

---

⁹ That is, *that I may reply to him who reproaches me.*

As teenagers, we are blessed to have friends who share our joys and challenges. Our friends are there to encourage us, support us, and lift us up when we need it most. However, Proverbs 27:11 reminds us of the importance of being a wise and discerning friend, and of the impact our friendships can have on those around us.

This proverb reminds us that being a wise and discerning friend can bring joy to the hearts of those around us. It encourages us to seek out friendships that bring joy and fulfillment to our lives, and to be willing to provide guidance and support to those who need it.

At the same time, this proverb also reminds us of the importance of being mindful of the impact our friendships can have on others. It encourages us to be wise and discerning in our relationships, and to be willing to stand up for our friends in the face of criticism or contempt.

So how can we be wise and discerning friends?

Firstly, we can be intentional about the friendships we form, seeking out those who share our values and beliefs and who encourage and support us in our faith.

Secondly, we can be willing to provide guidance and support to those who need it, offering a listening ear and a kind word when our friends are facing challenges or difficulties.

Lastly, we can be willing to stand up for our friends in the face of criticism or contempt, refusing to let others tear them down or speak ill of them.

So today, let's make a commitment to being wise and discerning friends. Let's seek out friendships that bring joy and fulfillment to our lives, provide guidance and support to those who need it, and stand up for our friends in the face of adversity. And as we do so, may we bring joy to the hearts of those around us and reflect God's love and compassion to those we encounter.

DAY 33 Seeking Wise Counsel

Proverbs 19:20 Updated American Standard Version (UASV)

²⁰ Listen to counsel and accept instruction,
   that you may gain wisdom in your end.[10]

Commentary

Proverbs 19:20 is a proverb that speaks to the importance of seeking wise counsel. The author writes, "Listen to advice and accept discipline, and at the end you will be counted among the wise."

This proverb reminds us of the importance of seeking out wise counsel in our lives. It speaks to the value of listening to the advice of others, even when it may be difficult to hear, and of being willing to accept discipline when it is necessary for our growth and development.

At the same time, this proverb also reminds us of the long-term benefits of seeking wise counsel. It encourages us to be patient and persistent in our pursuit of wisdom, knowing that it will ultimately lead us to a place of greater understanding and maturity.

Ultimately, Proverbs 19:20 is a powerful reminder of the importance of seeking wise counsel in our lives. It encourages us to be open to the advice of others, and to be willing to accept discipline when it is necessary for our growth and development. And as we do so, may we be counted among the wise and experience the fullness of life that comes from seeking God's wisdom and guidance.

Devotional for Youth

---

[10] That is, *in your future.*

As teenagers, we face a world filled with challenges and uncertainties. We are constantly making decisions that will shape our futures, and it can be difficult to know the right path to take. However, Proverbs 19:20 reminds us of the importance of seeking wise counsel, and of the value of listening to the advice of others.

This proverb reminds us that seeking out wise counsel is essential for our growth and development. It speaks to the importance of listening to the advice of others, even when it may be difficult to hear, and of being willing to accept discipline when it is necessary for our growth and maturity.

At the same time, this proverb also reminds us of the long-term benefits of seeking wise counsel. It encourages us to be patient and persistent in our pursuit of wisdom, knowing that it will ultimately lead us to a place of greater understanding and maturity.

So how can we seek wise counsel in our lives?

Firstly, we can seek out trusted mentors and role models who can offer guidance and support as we navigate life's challenges.

Secondly, we can be open to the advice of others, even when it may be difficult to hear or accept. We can recognize that we do not have all the answers, and be willing to learn from the experiences and wisdom of those around us.

Lastly, we can be willing to accept discipline when it is necessary for our growth and development. We can recognize that discipline is an essential part of our journey towards maturity, and be open to correction and guidance when it is needed.

So today, let's make a commitment to seeking wise counsel in our lives. Let's seek out mentors and role models who can offer guidance and support, be open to the advice of others, and be willing to accept discipline when it is necessary for our growth and development. And as we do so, may we be counted among the wise and experience the fullness of life that comes from seeking God's wisdom and guidance.

DAY 34 The Value of Diligence and Hard Work

Proverbs 12:24   Updated American Standard Version (UASV)

[24] The hand of the diligent will rule,
   while the slothful will be put to forced labor.

Commentary

Proverbs 12:24 is a proverb that speaks to the importance of diligence and hard work. The author writes, "Diligent hands will rule, but laziness ends in forced labor."

This proverb reminds us that diligence and hard work are essential for success in life. It speaks to the value of being committed and dedicated to our goals, and of the importance of putting in the effort required to achieve them.

At the same time, this proverb also warns us of the consequences of laziness and inaction. It reminds us that failing to work hard and be diligent in our pursuits can lead to negative consequences, such as being forced into labor or missing out on opportunities for growth and development.

Ultimately, Proverbs 12:24 is a powerful reminder of the importance of diligence and hard work in our lives. It encourages us to be committed and dedicated to our goals, and to be willing to put in the effort required to achieve them. And as we do so, may we experience the fullness of life that comes from being diligent and hardworking in all that we do.

Devotional for Youth

As teenagers, we are at a point in our lives where we are beginning to discover our passions and pursue our goals. However, pursuing these goals can be challenging, and it can be difficult to

101

know how to achieve them. Proverbs 12:24 reminds us of the importance of diligence and hard work, and of the value of being committed and dedicated to our pursuits.

This proverb reminds us that diligent hands will rule, and that hard work is essential for success in life. It speaks to the value of being committed and dedicated to our goals, and of the importance of putting in the effort required to achieve them.

At the same time, this proverb also warns us of the consequences of laziness and inaction. It reminds us that failing to work hard and be diligent in our pursuits can lead to negative consequences, such as being forced into labor or missing out on opportunities for growth and development.

So how can we be diligent and hardworking in our pursuits?

Firstly, we can set clear goals for ourselves, and be intentional about the steps we take to achieve them. We can be committed and dedicated to our goals, and be willing to put in the effort required to achieve them.

Secondly, we can be mindful of the consequences of laziness and inaction and recognize that hard work is essential for success in life. We can be willing to take responsibility for our actions and be willing to put in the effort required to achieve our goals.

Lastly, we can seek out the guidance and support of others as we pursue our goals. We can recognize that we do not have all the answers and be open to the wisdom and experience of those around us.

So today, let's make a commitment to diligence and hard work in our pursuits. Let's be committed and dedicated to our goals, be mindful of the consequences of laziness and inaction, and seek out the guidance and support of others as we pursue our passions. And as we do so, may we experience the fullness of life that comes from being diligent and hardworking in all that we do.

DAY 35 The Value of Wisdom and Knowledge

Proverbs 2:9 Updated American Standard Version (UASV)

⁹ Then you will understand righteousness and justice
and equity, every good course;

Commentary

Proverbs 2:9 is a powerful reminder of the value of wisdom and knowledge. The author writes, "Then you will understand what is right and just and fair—every good path."

This proverb reminds us that wisdom and knowledge are essential for living a righteous and just life. It speaks to the importance of understanding what is right and fair, and of being committed to following the path that leads to righteousness and justice.

At the same time, this proverb also reminds us that wisdom and knowledge are not things that can be obtained easily. It speaks to the importance of seeking out wisdom and knowledge, and of being committed to the pursuit of understanding.

Ultimately, Proverbs 2:9 is a powerful reminder of the importance of wisdom and knowledge in our lives. It encourages us to be committed to the pursuit of understanding, and to be mindful of the ways in which wisdom and knowledge can help us to live a righteous and just life. And as we seek out wisdom and knowledge, may we experience the fullness of life that comes from living in alignment with God's will and purpose.

Devotional for Youth

As teenagers, we are at a point in our lives where we are beginning to make important decisions about our futures. We may be deciding on a career path, choosing which college to attend, or even considering our values and beliefs. In the midst of all of these decisions, it can be easy to feel overwhelmed and unsure of the right path to take. But Proverbs 2:9 reminds us of the value of wisdom and knowledge, and of the importance of seeking understanding as we navigate the complexities of life.

This proverb speaks to the importance of understanding what is right and just and fair, and of being committed to following the path that leads to righteousness and justice. It reminds us that wisdom and knowledge are essential for living a righteous and just life, and that we must be intentional about seeking out understanding if we are to navigate the complexities of life successfully.

At the same time, this proverb also reminds us that wisdom and knowledge are not things that can be obtained easily. It speaks to the importance of seeking out wisdom and knowledge, and of being committed to the pursuit of understanding. It encourages us to be open to learning from others, to seek out guidance and support, and to be committed to the journey of growth and development.

So how can we seek out wisdom and knowledge as we navigate the complexities of life?

Firstly, we can be intentional about seeking out knowledge through reading, research, and conversation with others. We can be open to learning from those who have more experience than us, and be willing to ask questions and seek guidance as we make decisions.

Secondly, we can be mindful of the values and beliefs that guide us, and seek out wisdom from God's word as we navigate the complexities of life. We can be committed to prayer and meditation, and seek guidance from God as we make decisions.

Lastly, we can seek out the support and guidance of others as we pursue our goals. We can surround ourselves with people who are committed to growth and development and be open to learning from their experiences and wisdom.

So today, let's make a commitment to seeking out wisdom and knowledge as we navigate the complexities of life. Let's be intentional about seeking out understanding, be mindful of the values and beliefs that guide us and seek out the support and guidance of others as we pursue our goals. And as we do so, may we experience the fullness of life that comes from living in alignment with God's will and purpose.

DAY 36 The Value of Wisdom

Proverbs 8:35-36   Updated American Standard Version (UASV)

³⁵ For whoever finds me finds life
  and obtains favor from Jehovah,
³⁶ But he who misses me injures his own soul;
  all those who hate me love death."

Commentary

Proverbs 8:35-36 speaks to the value of wisdom and the rewards that come with seeking it. The author writes, "For those who find me find life and receive favor from the Lord. But those who fail to find me harm themselves; all who hate me love death."

This proverb reminds us that wisdom is a valuable and life-giving pursuit, and that seeking it is essential for experiencing the fullness of life that God intends for us. It speaks to the rewards that come with seeking wisdom, and of the favor that God extends to those who are committed to the pursuit of understanding.

At the same time, this proverb also warns us of the consequences of failing to seek wisdom. It reminds us that failing to pursue understanding can lead to harm and even death, and that we must be intentional about seeking out wisdom if we are to experience the fullness of life that God intends for us.

Ultimately, Proverbs 8:35-36 is a powerful reminder of the value of wisdom and the rewards that come with seeking it. It encourages us to be committed to the pursuit of understanding, and to be mindful of the ways in which wisdom can help us to live a full and abundant life. And as we seek out wisdom, may we experience the favor and blessings that come with aligning our lives with God's will and purpose.

Devotional for Youth

As teenagers, we are at a point in our lives where we are beginning to make important decisions that will shape our future. It can be challenging to navigate the complexities of life and to make decisions that align with God's will and purpose. But Proverbs 8:35-36 reminds us of the value of wisdom and of the importance of seeking it as we navigate the complexities of life.

This proverb speaks to the value of wisdom and the rewards that come with seeking it. It reminds us that those who find wisdom find life and receive favor from the Lord. Seeking wisdom is essential for experiencing the fullness of life that God intends for us. It helps us to make wise decisions, to navigate challenging situations, and to live in alignment with God's will and purpose.

At the same time, this proverb also warns us of the consequences of failing to seek wisdom. It reminds us that failing to pursue understanding can lead to harm and even death, and that we must be intentional about seeking out wisdom if we are to experience the fullness of life that God intends for us.

So how can we seek out wisdom as we navigate the complexities of life?

Firstly, we can seek out guidance from God's word through prayer and meditation. We can be intentional about studying the Bible, seeking out understanding, and applying its teachings to our lives.

Secondly, we can be open to learning from others, seeking out guidance and support from those who have more experience than us. We can be willing to ask questions, seek advice, and learn from the wisdom of others.

Lastly, we can be committed to the pursuit of understanding, seeking out knowledge through reading, research, and conversation with others. We can be open to new ideas, be willing to challenge our assumptions, and be committed to the journey of growth and development.

So today, let's make a commitment to seeking out wisdom as we navigate the complexities of life. Let's be intentional about seeking out understanding, be open to learning from others, and be committed to the pursuit of knowledge. And as we do so, may we experience the fullness of life that comes from living in alignment with God's will and purpose.

DAY 37 Trusting in God's Plan

Proverbs 19:21 Updated American Standard Version (UASV)

²¹ Many are the plans in the heart of a man,
   but it is the purpose of Jehovah that will stand.

Commentary

Proverbs 19:21 states, "Many are the plans in a person's heart, but it is the Lord's purpose that prevails." This proverb reminds us that although we may have plans and desires for our lives, ultimately, it is God's plan that will prevail.

The verse speaks to the importance of aligning our plans and desires with God's will, recognizing that our own plans may not always align with his purpose. We may have our own ideas about what our lives should look like, but it is ultimately God's plan for us that will lead us to the greatest fulfillment and purpose.

This proverb also speaks to the sovereignty of God, reminding us that he is in control and that his plan will ultimately prevail. We can take comfort in knowing that even when our plans don't work out, God's plan for our lives is still at work, leading us toward his ultimate purpose.

Ultimately, Proverbs 19:21 reminds us to trust in God's plan for our lives, to seek his will and purpose, and to be open to the ways in which he is guiding us toward our ultimate calling and destiny. We can take comfort in knowing that even when things don't go as planned, God's plan for our lives is still at work, leading us toward his ultimate purpose.

Devotional for Youth

As teenagers, we often have plans and dreams for our future. We may have ideas about what we want to do, who we want to be, and what we hope to achieve. But Proverbs 19:21 reminds us that although we may have plans, it is ultimately God's purpose that will prevail.

This proverb speaks to the importance of aligning our plans and desires with God's will, recognizing that our own plans may not always align with his purpose. It reminds us that even when things don't go as planned, God's plan for our lives is still at work, leading us toward his ultimate purpose.

So how can we trust in God's plan for our lives, even when things don't go as planned?

Firstly, we can seek God's guidance and direction through prayer and meditation. We can be intentional about seeking his will and purpose for our lives, asking for guidance and direction as we make important decisions.

Secondly, we can be open to the ways in which God is guiding us, even when it may not be what we expected or wanted. We can trust that he is working all things together for our good, even when we don't understand how.

Lastly, we can be committed to living in alignment with God's will and purpose, even when it may not be easy or popular. We can be willing to let go of our own plans and desires, trusting that God's plan for our lives is ultimately the best plan.

So today, let's commit to trusting in God's plan for our lives, even when things don't go as planned. Let's seek his guidance and direction, be open to his leading, and be committed to living in alignment with his will and purpose. And as we do so, may we experience the fullness of life that comes from trusting in the sovereign plan of our loving God.

DAY 38 Kindness Can Heal Anxiety

Proverbs 12:25 Updated American Standard Version (UASV)

²⁵ Anxiety in a man's heart weighs him down,
  but a good word makes him glad.

Commentary

Proverbs 12:25 states, "Anxiety weighs down the heart, but a kind word cheers it up." This proverb highlights the power of words to affect our emotional well-being. It recognizes that anxiety and worry can be heavy burdens that weigh us down, but that kind and encouraging words can lift our spirits and bring joy to our hearts.

This verse speaks to the importance of the words we use, and the impact they can have on others. It reminds us that our words have the power to build others up or tear them down, and that we should be intentional about using them to bring encouragement and comfort to those around us.

Additionally, this proverb highlights the importance of kindness in our interactions with others. It reminds us that a simple act of kindness, such as a kind word or a thoughtful gesture, can make a world of difference to someone who is struggling with anxiety or worry.

Ultimately, Proverbs 12:25 reminds us to be mindful of the words we use, and to be intentional about using them to bring encouragement and comfort to those around us. It also reminds us of the power of kindness and the difference it can make in the lives of others. As we strive to live out this verse, may we be a source of comfort and encouragement to those around us, and may we bring joy and peace to those who are burdened with anxiety and worry.

Devotional for Youth

As teenagers, we often experience anxiety and worry about various aspects of our lives - our grades, friendships, relationships, future plans, and so on. Anxiety can be a heavy burden that weighs us down and affects our emotional well-being. But Proverbs 12:25 reminds us that a kind word can lift our spirits and bring joy to our hearts.

This verse highlights the power of kindness in our interactions with others. It reminds us that a simple act of kindness, such as a kind word or a thoughtful gesture, can make a world of difference to someone who is struggling with anxiety or worry. It reminds us that we can be a source of comfort and encouragement to those around us simply by being kind and thoughtful.

But Proverbs 12:25 also speaks to the importance of being mindful of the words we use. It reminds us that our words have the power to build others up or tear them down, and that we should be intentional about using them to bring encouragement and comfort to those around us.

So how can we show kindness to those who are struggling with anxiety?

Firstly, we can be intentional about speaking kind and uplifting words to those around us. We can take the time to express our appreciation for them, to acknowledge their strengths and talents, and to offer words of encouragement and hope.

Secondly, we can be thoughtful in our actions, taking the time to show care and compassion for those who are struggling. We can offer a listening ear, a shoulder to cry on, or a helping hand when needed.

Lastly, we can pray for those who are struggling with anxiety, asking God to bring them comfort, peace, and hope. We can also ask God to show us ways to be a source of comfort and encouragement to those around us who may be struggling.

So today, let's commit to showing kindness to those who are struggling with anxiety. Let's be intentional about using our words and actions to bring comfort and encouragement to those around us, and let's pray for those who may be struggling. As we do so, may we be a reflection of Christ's love and compassion, and may we bring healing and hope to those who are burdened with anxiety and worry.

Day 39 True Wealth and Prosperity

Proverbs 10:22 Updated American Standard Version (UASV)

²² The blessing of Jehovah, it makes rich,
and he adds no sorrow to it.

Commentary

Proverbs 10:22 states, "The blessing of the Lord makes rich, and he adds no sorrow with it." This verse reminds us that true wealth and prosperity come from God's blessings, and that these blessings bring joy and peace without any sorrow or pain.

In the context of the book of Proverbs, this verse highlights the importance of wisdom and righteousness in our pursuit of wealth and prosperity. It emphasizes that true wealth and prosperity come not from material possessions, but from God's blessings on our lives. It also reminds us that God's blessings bring true joy and peace, and that we should seek to live our lives in a way that honors Him and invites His blessings into our lives.

Furthermore, this verse speaks to the nature of God's blessings. It emphasizes that God's blessings are not accompanied by sorrow or pain, and that they bring true joy and peace to our lives. It reminds us that the blessings of the Lord are a source of comfort and encouragement, and that they sustain us through the ups and downs of life.

Ultimately, Proverbs 10:22 encourages us to seek God's blessings in our lives, and to trust in His provision and care. It reminds us that true wealth and prosperity come from God's blessings, and that we should seek to live our lives in a way that invites His blessings into our lives. As we do so, may we experience the true joy and peace that come from God's blessings, and may we be a blessing to others as we share the abundance of His grace and love.

Devotional for Youth

As teenagers, we often desire to be rich and prosperous. We dream of a life filled with material possessions, financial stability, and worldly success. But Proverbs 10:22 reminds us that true wealth and prosperity come from God's blessings, and that they bring joy and peace without any sorrow or pain.

This verse challenges us to examine our understanding of wealth and prosperity. It reminds us that true wealth and prosperity are not measured by the number of possessions we have, but by the blessings of the Lord on our lives. It challenges us to reorient our priorities and to seek God's blessings above all else.

But Proverbs 10:22 also speaks to the nature of God's blessings. It reminds us that His blessings bring true joy and peace, and that they sustain us through the ups and downs of life. It emphasizes that God's blessings are not accompanied by sorrow or pain, but rather by a deep sense of contentment and gratitude.

So how can we seek God's blessings in our lives?

Firstly, we can seek to live our lives in a way that honors God and invites His blessings. We can strive to cultivate a heart of gratitude and contentment, focusing on the blessings that He has already given us and trusting in His provision for our future.

Secondly, we can seek to use the blessings that God has given us to bless others. We can use our resources, talents, and time to serve others, to share the love of Christ, and to make a positive impact on the world around us.

Lastly, we can seek to cultivate a heart of generosity, recognizing that the blessings of the Lord are meant to be shared with others. We can seek to be a blessing to those around us, using our resources to meet the needs of others and to make a difference in the world.

So today, let's seek true wealth and prosperity through God's blessings. Let's focus on cultivating a heart of gratitude and contentment, and let's use the blessings that God has given us to bless others. As we do so, may we experience the true joy and peace that come from God's blessings, and may we be a blessing to others as we share the abundance of His grace and love.

DAY 40 Walking with the Wise

Proverbs 13:20 Updated American Standard Version (UASV)

²⁰ He who walks with wise men will be wise,
  but the companion of fools will suffer harm.

Commentary

Proverbs 13:20 says, "Whoever walks with the wise becomes wise, but the companion of fools will suffer harm." This verse reminds us that the people we choose to associate with can have a significant impact on our lives, and that our relationships can either lead us towards wisdom or towards harm.

The first half of this verse emphasizes the importance of surrounding ourselves with wise and godly people. It highlights the fact that we can learn from the wisdom and experience of those who have gone before us, and that their influence can help us to grow in our own wisdom and understanding.

The second half of this verse serves as a warning against choosing the wrong kind of companions. It reminds us that those who associate with foolish or unwise people may suffer harm as a result, either from the negative influence of their companions or from the consequences of their own poor choices.

Ultimately, this verse encourages us to be intentional about the people we choose to associate with. It challenges us to seek out wise and godly mentors and friends who can help us to grow in our faith and wisdom, and to avoid those who might lead us towards harm.

Furthermore, this verse reminds us that we have a responsibility to be a positive influence on those around us. It encourages us to be a wise and godly companion to others, to share our own wisdom and experience with those who might benefit from it, and to be a positive influence on the world around us.

May we be intentional about the company we keep, seeking out wise and godly companions who can help us to grow in our faith and wisdom, and may we also seek to be a positive influence on others as we share the wisdom and love of Christ with those around us.

Devotional for Youth

As teenagers, we are constantly surrounded by people who influence us. Whether it's our friends, family members, or social media, the people we associate with have a powerful impact on our thoughts, beliefs, and actions.

Proverbs 13:20 reminds us of the importance of surrounding ourselves with wise and godly people. It highlights the fact that the company we keep can either lead us towards wisdom and growth or towards harm and destruction.

This verse challenges us to be intentional about the people we choose to associate with. It encourages us to seek out wise and godly mentors and friends who can help us to grow in our faith and understanding of God's Word.

But what does it mean to "walk with the wise?" It means more than just spending time with people who are knowledgeable or successful. It means seeking out people who have a deep love for God and who are committed to living out His Word in their lives.

Walking with the wise means listening to their advice, learning from their experiences, and allowing them to challenge us to grow in our faith and understanding. It means being humble enough to admit that we don't have all the answers and that we need the wisdom and guidance of others.

On the other hand, the second half of this verse warns us about the dangers of associating with fools. It reminds us that those who surround themselves with unwise or foolish people may suffer harm as a result.

This doesn't mean that we should avoid all contact with those who are unwise or foolish. Instead, it means that we should be discerning about the kind of influence they have on our lives and seek to be a positive influence on them as well.

As we seek to follow Christ and grow in our faith, let's be intentional about the people we choose to associate with. Let's seek out wise and godly mentors and friends who can help us to grow in our faith and understanding, and let's also seek to be a positive influence on those around us as we share the love and wisdom of Christ with others.

APPENDIX A How Can I Resist Peer Pressure?

As a teenager, you face a lot of different pressures in your life. One of the biggest challenges you may encounter is peer pressure. This can come in many different forms, from pressure to fit in with a certain group to pressure to engage in risky behaviors or activities.

It can be tough to stand up to peer pressure, but it's important to remember that you have the power to make your own choices and decisions. Here are some ways that teenagers can resist peer pressure today:

1. Know your values and beliefs

The first step in resisting peer pressure is to know your own values and beliefs. Take some time to reflect on what is important to you and what you believe in. This will help you to make decisions that align with your values and avoid behaviors that go against them.

2. Surround yourself with positive influences

It's important to surround yourself with positive influences, such as friends and family members who support and encourage you. Seek out people who share your values and who will lift you up instead of bringing you down.

3. Practice saying no

Learning to say no is an important skill for resisting peer pressure. Practice saying no in different situations so that you feel confident in your ability to stand up for yourself. Remember that you don't have to give in to pressure just to fit in with a group.

4. Make a plan

If you know you'll be in a situation where you may face peer pressure, make a plan ahead of time for how you'll handle it. For example, if you're going to a party where there may be alcohol, decide ahead of time that you won't drink and plan to leave if you feel uncomfortable.

5. Use humor

Sometimes using humor can be a way to diffuse a situation and resist peer pressure. If someone is pressuring you to do something you don't want to do, try using humor to deflect the pressure and change the subject.

6. Focus on the long-term

When facing peer pressure, it can be tempting to focus on the short-term benefits of fitting in with a group. But it's important to remember that the decisions you make now can have long-term consequences. Focus on the big picture and think about how your choices today will impact your future.

7. Seek help if needed

If you're struggling to resist peer pressure or feel overwhelmed by it, don't be afraid to seek help. Talk to a trusted adult, such as a parent, teacher, or counselor, who can provide guidance and support.

In conclusion, resisting peer pressure can be a challenge, but it's important to remember that you have the power to make your own choices and decisions. By knowing your values and beliefs, surrounding yourself with positive influences, practicing saying no, making a plan, using humor, focusing on the long-term, and seeking help if needed, you can resist peer pressure and stay true to yourself.

APPENDIX B Why Do I Get So Depressed?

Depression is a serious mental health condition that affects millions of people around the world, including teenagers. It can cause feelings of sadness, hopelessness, and loss of interest in activities that used to bring joy. Coping with depression can be a challenging experience for anyone, but it can be particularly difficult for teenagers who may be dealing with the pressures of school, social relationships, and other life changes.

If you're a teenager who is struggling with depression, it's important to know that you're not alone and that help is available. Here are some ways that teenagers can cope with depression today:

1.   Seek professional help

The first and most important step in coping with depression is to seek professional help. Talk to your parents, a trusted adult, or a healthcare provider about how you're feeling. They can provide guidance and support, and may refer you to a mental health professional who can help you develop a treatment plan.

2.   Practice self-care

Taking care of your physical and emotional needs is an important part of coping with depression. This includes getting enough sleep, eating a healthy diet, and engaging in regular physical activity. You may also find it helpful to engage in relaxation techniques, such as yoga or meditation, to help reduce stress and promote relaxation.

3.   Build a support network

Having a supportive network of friends and family members can be a valuable resource when coping with depression. Reach out to people you trust and talk to them about how you're feeling. You may also consider joining a support group for teens with depression.

4.   Set realistic goals

Depression can make it difficult to focus on daily tasks and responsibilities. Setting realistic goals for yourself can help you stay motivated and give you a sense of accomplishment. Start with small goals, such as getting out of bed in the morning or completing one task per day, and gradually work your way up to bigger goals.

5. Challenge negative thoughts

Negative thoughts are a common symptom of depression. Learning to recognize and challenge negative thoughts can help you develop a more positive outlook. When you have a negative thought, try to challenge it by asking yourself if it's really true or if there's another way to look at the situation.

6. Engage in meaningful activities

Engaging in activities that bring you joy and fulfillment can help lift your mood and promote a sense of well-being. This may include creative pursuits, such as art or music, or activities that involve helping others, such as volunteering.

7. Avoid substance use

Using drugs or alcohol to cope with depression can actually make your symptoms worse and increase your risk of developing a substance use disorder. If you're struggling with substance use, seek help from a healthcare professional or addiction specialist.

8. Stay connected with others

Depression can cause you to withdraw from social situations, but staying connected with others can be an important part of coping with the condition. Make an effort to stay connected with friends and family members, even if it's just through phone or video calls.

9. Learn relaxation techniques

Relaxation techniques, such as deep breathing, progressive muscle relaxation, and visualization, can help reduce stress and promote relaxation. Practice these techniques regularly to help manage symptoms of depression.

10. Be patient with yourself

Coping with depression can be a long and challenging process. Be patient with yourself and remember that recovery takes time. Celebrate your small victories and don't be too hard on yourself if you have setbacks.

In conclusion, coping with depression can be a difficult journey, but it's important to remember that help is available and that recovery is possible. By seeking professional help, practicing self-care, building a support network, setting realistic goals, challenging negative thoughts, engaging in meaningful activities, avoiding substance use, staying connected with others, learning relaxation techniques, and being patient with yourself, you can take steps toward managing your symptoms of depression and improving your overall well-being.

APPENDIX C Why Am I So Stressed?

Stress is a natural part of life, and as teenagers, you are likely to experience it in various aspects of your life. Whether it's due to academic pressure, social obligations, family problems, or other life challenges, stress can be overwhelming and can affect your mental and physical health. However, there are ways to cope with stress and manage it effectively. In this article, we will discuss some strategies that can help teenagers cope with stress in today's world.

1. Identify the sources of stress

The first step in coping with stress is to identify the sources of stress. Understanding what triggers stress can help you develop a plan to manage it. Take some time to reflect on what situations or events make you feel stressed. It could be academic pressure, peer pressure, relationship problems, or family issues. Once you identify the sources of stress, you can develop a plan to address them.

2. Practice mindfulness

Mindfulness is the practice of being present in the moment and paying attention to your thoughts, feelings, and sensations without judgment. Mindfulness can help reduce stress and increase resilience. There are several mindfulness techniques that you can try, such as deep breathing, meditation, and yoga. These techniques can help you stay calm and focused when you are feeling stressed.

3. Develop a healthy lifestyle

A healthy lifestyle is important in managing stress. Eating a balanced diet, getting enough sleep, and engaging in regular physical activity can help reduce stress levels. Exercise releases endorphins, which are natural mood-boosters that can help you feel more relaxed and energized. Developing healthy habits can also help you build resilience, which can help you manage stress more effectively.

4. Learn time management skills

Time management skills are essential in managing stress. Poor time management can lead to procrastination, which can cause stress levels to escalate. It is important to prioritize your tasks and set realistic goals. Break down larger tasks into smaller, more manageable ones, and allocate time for each task. By managing your time effectively, you can reduce stress and feel more in control of your life.

5.   Develop a support network

Having a support network of family and friends is essential in coping with stress. Talking to someone you trust can help you feel heard and understood. You can also seek support from a counselor or mental health professional if you need help managing stress. There are also online support groups and forums that can connect you with people who are going through similar experiences.

6.   Avoid negative coping mechanisms

When under stress, it can be tempting to turn to negative coping mechanisms such as alcohol, drugs, or binge-eating. These coping mechanisms may provide temporary relief, but they can lead to more problems in the long run. Instead, focus on healthy coping mechanisms such as exercise, meditation, or spending time with friends and family.

7.   Engage in activities that bring joy

Engaging in activities that bring joy can help reduce stress and improve your overall well-being. This could be anything from reading a book, listening to music, or spending time outdoors. Finding activities that you enjoy can help you relax and take your mind off of stressful situations.

In conclusion, stress is a natural part of life, but it doesn't have to control you. By identifying the sources of stress, practicing mindfulness, developing a healthy lifestyle, learning time management skills, building a support network, avoiding negative coping mechanisms, and engaging in activities that bring joy, you can effectively manage stress and improve your overall well-being. Remember that managing stress is a journey, and it takes time and practice. Be patient with yourself, and don't hesitate to seek help if you need it.

APPENDIX D How Can I Protect Myself from Bullying and Cyberbullying

Bullying and cyberbullying can have devastating effects on teenagers. It can cause emotional distress, physical harm, and affect academic performance. However, there are ways to protect yourself from bullying and cyberbullying. In this article, we will discuss some strategies that can help teenagers protect themselves from bullying and cyberbullying in today's world. We will also discuss how physical fitness and unarmed self-defense can be incorporated into these strategies.

1. Recognize the signs of bullying

The first step in protecting yourself from bullying is to recognize the signs. This includes physical aggression, verbal abuse, exclusion from social groups, and cyberbullying. It is essential to understand that bullying can take various forms, and it is not limited to physical harm. Once you recognize the signs, you can take action to protect yourself.

2. Seek support from trusted individuals

It is important to seek support from trusted individuals when dealing with bullying. This includes parents, teachers, counselors, and friends. These individuals can provide emotional support, advice, and intervene when necessary. Building a support network can also help you feel less isolated and more confident in dealing with bullying.

3. Avoid responding to cyberbullying

Cyberbullying can be challenging to deal with because it can occur anonymously and can spread quickly. It is essential to avoid responding to cyberbullying and to report it to the appropriate authorities. This includes social media platforms, school administrators, or law enforcement. Responding to cyberbullying can escalate the situation, and it can also affect your mental health.

4. Practice physical fitness

Physical fitness can help build confidence and resilience, which can help protect you from bullying. Engage in regular physical activity such as running, swimming, or weightlifting. Physical activity can also help reduce stress and anxiety, which can be beneficial in dealing with bullying.

5. Learn unarmed self-defense

Learning unarmed self-defense can provide you with practical skills to protect yourself from physical harm. It is essential to seek training from a qualified instructor and to practice regularly. Self-defense can also provide you with a sense of empowerment and confidence.

6. Seek professional help

Dealing with bullying can be emotionally challenging, and it is essential to seek professional help if necessary. This includes counseling or therapy from a qualified mental health professional. Professional help can provide you with the tools and strategies to cope with bullying effectively.

In conclusion, protecting yourself from bullying and cyberbullying requires awareness, support, and practical skills. Recognizing the signs of bullying, seeking support from trusted individuals, avoiding responding to cyberbullying, practicing physical fitness, learning unarmed self-defense, and seeking professional help are effective strategies to protect yourself. It is essential to remember that dealing with bullying can be challenging, but it is possible to overcome it with the right tools and support.

APPENDIX E How Can I Help My Friends Who Are Struggling with the Difficulties of Being a Teen Today?

Being a teenager can be challenging, and it is common for friends to struggle with various concerns and challenges. As a friend, it is essential to provide support and help your friend navigate these difficulties. In this article, we will discuss some practical ways a teenager can help their friends who are struggling with the concerns and challenges of being a teen.

1. Listen and validate their feelings

The first step in helping a friend is to listen and validate their feelings. This means allowing your friend to express their concerns and emotions without judgment. It is essential to validate their feelings by acknowledging their experiences and letting them know that you understand what they are going through.

2. Offer support and encouragement

Offering support and encouragement is another way to help your friend. This includes being there for them when they need to talk or vent their feelings. You can also offer words of encouragement, such as letting them know that you believe in them and their abilities. It is essential to let your friend know that they are not alone and that you are there to support them.

3. Help them find resources

If your friend is struggling with a particular issue, such as mental health or academic difficulties, it is important to help them find resources. This includes researching resources such as counseling services, academic support programs, or community organizations that can provide support. You can also accompany your friend to appointments or support groups.

4. Encourage healthy habits

Encouraging healthy habits is another way to help your friend. This includes encouraging them to eat well, exercise, get enough sleep, and avoid harmful behaviors such as drug or alcohol use.

You can also engage in healthy activities together, such as going for a walk or trying a new healthy recipe.

5. Be patient and non-judgmental

It is essential to be patient and non-judgmental when helping your friend. Remember that everyone deals with challenges differently, and it may take time for your friend to overcome their difficulties. Avoid being critical or judgmental, and instead, offer support and understanding.

6. Set boundaries

While it is important to be there for your friend, it is also important to set boundaries. This means recognizing your limits and not taking on more than you can handle. It is also essential to take care of yourself and not neglect your own needs while helping your friend.

7. Seek help if necessary

If your friend is struggling with a severe issue such as self-harm, substance abuse, or suicidal thoughts, it is important to seek help immediately. This includes reaching out to a trusted adult, such as a teacher, counselor, or parent, or contacting a crisis hotline.

In conclusion, helping a friend who is struggling with the concerns and challenges of being a teen requires compassion, patience, and practical support. Listening and validating their feelings, offering support and encouragement, helping them find resources, encouraging healthy habits, being patient and non-judgmental, setting boundaries, and seeking help if necessary are practical ways to help your friend. Remember that being a supportive friend can make a significant difference in someone's life, and it is important to be there for your friends during difficult times.